SHAMAN'S BLUES
THE ART & INFLUENCES BEHIND JIM MORRISON & THE DOORS

SHAMAN'S BLUES: THE ART AND
INFLUENCES BEHIND JIM MORRISON
AND THE DOORS
Copyright © 2014 Denise Sullivan

Published by:
Sumach-Red Books

an imprint of Blooming Twig Books
New York / Tulsa
www.bloomingtwig.com

San Francisco designer Barbara Stauffacher Solomon conceived the cover. A pioneer of supergraphics, Swiss-trained Barbara brought clear design elements to the US in the late '50s and early '60s. She designed many of the New Directions paperbacks Jim Morrison enjoyed upon first publication. Barbara knew exactly what the book should look like, and the same may be said of Laurie Sheets Forbes, an award-winning San Francisco designer who oversaw computer graphics, color, and back cover art direction.

The cover photo by Yale Joel is from a
1968 unpublished session for *Life* Magazine.
It is reprinted with permission of Photofest.

All rights reserved. This book may not be photocopied for personal or professional use. No part of this book may be reproduced, stored in a retrieval system, or transmitted in any form or by any means (electronic, mechanical, photocopying, recording, or otherwise) without permission in writing from the author and/or publisher.

Hardcover ISBN 978-1-937753-03-0
Paperback ISBN 978-1-937753-04-7
eBook ISBN 978-1-937753-05-4

First edition.

Also by Denise Sullivan

R.E.M. Talk About the Passion

Rip It Up: Rock'n'Roll Rulebreakers

The White Stripes: Sweethearts of the Blues

Keep on Pushing: Black Power Music From Blues to Hip Hop

SHAMAN'S BLUES
THE ART & INFLUENCES BEHIND JIM MORRISON & THE DOORS
DENISE SULLIVAN

To my pal Bette — Thanks for being a strong support! Denise 2014.

2014

Sumach-Red Books

New York / Tulsa

*There can't be any large-scale revolution until there's
a personal revolution, on an individual level.
It's got to happen inside first.*

–Jim Morrison

TABLE OF CONTENTS

Introduction	i
1. This is the End: 1964-1965	17
2. Santa Monica, Venice, and The Doors of Perception: 1965-1966	35
3. Sunset Strip: 1966-1967	63
4. Strange Days Have Found Him: 1967	75
5. Shaman's Blues: 1968	87
6. Paradise Lost: 1969	119
7. Back to Basics: 1969-1970	139
8. LA Women: 1970-1971	153
9. Au Revoir LA: 1971	163
10. Since Then: 1971-2013	171
Acknowledgments	191
Notes	193
Bibliography	205

INTRODUCTION

"A child is like a flower, whose head is just floating in the breeze," once said Jim Morrison. Driving through the New Mexico desert at dawn, he believed he was just three, maybe four, when his family encountered the accident scene. The only story with any consistent detail that survives his youth, it is the substance of his poem, "Dawn's Highway" the interlude of the Doors' song "Peace Frog," and is referenced in stories and especially jokes, about the shaman and his appropriation of Native ideas.

Indians scattered
on dawn's highway bleeding,
ghosts cloud the young
child's eggshell mind

The incident goes some way toward explaining why Morrison was the way he was – extreme, haunted, stimulated by trauma and dreams, a lover of earth and sky, animals and people, moved to create something beautiful, little gifts left along the trail to be discovered, over time. A free spirit, bound to ancient ritual, he found his tribe among a feast of friends in late '50s and mid '60s California, the far western edge of the world, the wild frontier's end of the line – *Land's end. Land ho!*

Though outside this one mystical event, Morrison rarely offered personal recollections of his past. "Dead" is what he said when asked of his family's status. When it was found they were in fact alive, he admitted that he'd lied. "I just didn't want to involve them," he said. "It's easy enough to find out personal details if you really want them." The family, in turn, were tight-lipped about their famous son, as if it was his destiny to arrive transfigured – like a God reborn, his mysteries to be witnessed and experienced, then pondered, perhaps even worshiped, until the end.

Born in Melbourne, Florida on December 8, 1943, James Douglas was the first boy of a naval man, Steve, and his wife, Clara Clarke Morrison. According to the timeline in his mind, Indian workers at the side of the road leapt into his soul sometime before the birth of his sister Anne in Albuquerque in 1947, and definitely before his brother Andy was born in Los Altos, California, in 1948. "It's not a ghost story man…it's something that really means something to me," he said.

In 1955, when Jim was 12, the Morrisons were transferred to Alameda, the Bay Area's naval air station. Living at 1717 Alameda Avenue, he entered middle school, developed his reputation as class clown, and tuned into movies, poetry, and music – Chuck Berry, Little Richard, and Fats Domino. Though moved by Elvis Presley, he didn't join a band like most musicians of the future would, though he said Bo Diddley saved his life with a song. Of far more interest to Jim was *Rebel Without A Cause*. He shared basic traits with Jimbo, James Dean's anti-hero, and took the actor's death at 24 like a personal blow. He loved Dean's final film, *Giant*, concerning big oil, race, and class in Texas, a place he got to know from listening to its big beat on late night radio.

Shopping for books and records in Oakland, he hunted for recordings by Welsh poet Dylan Thomas and American humorist Lenny Bruce, while snapping up discs by John Lee Hooker, and electric bluesmen Muddy Waters and Howlin' Wolf, with their songs by Willie Dixon, the basis for the world's greatest rock 'n' roll. He noticed the way their words created an incantatory effect, and it was an idea with which he would become increasingly obsessed.

As the rhythm of language howled for Jim, he answered the call, reaching for the world disassembling, just outside his door: Allen Ginsberg was writing in Berkeley, and in San Francisco there was a poetry renaissance afoot. Following the publication of *Howl* and its highly publicized obscenity trial, Jim boldly staked out the City Lights store, a trip that bookmarked his fascination with all things Beat. Hoping to meet a poet, he bumped into Lawrence Ferlinghetti there, though he stumbled and retreated, in a fit of shyness.

Back home in Alameda, Jim had made friends – guys with whom he played baseball and swam, who shared his *MAD* magazine sense of humor, teenage obsession with girls, and a taste for adventure inspired by Jack Kerouac. Drawing in sketchbooks, tinkering with home recordings with comedic and satirical flair, he lampooned life behind the idyll curtain and learned to cope. In Alameda, Jimmy, as he was known, was becoming Jim Morrison. Meanwhile his father, rising through ranks to Rear Admiral, had returned from naval operations to spend more time at home. Jim would pay dearly for his missteps on board the USS Morrison, but that ship had already sailed: By age 15, following residency in four states and three California towns, discipline was officially a problem.

In late 1958, the family once again relocated, this time to Alexandria, Virginia, where a heartsick Jim finished high school in 1959. Later that year, Marlon Brando appeared in *The Fugitive Kind*. A fox in a henhouse is what Tennessee Williams called his Orpheus in snakeskin character, a loner with a passion for art, a vagabond with a lust for life. It was a role that appealed to Jim, as he blew like a tornado from town to town, bearing chaos with each landing.

Teachers began to report moods – skittish, anti-social, uncooperative. Something strange came over Jim. His unease culminated in a near-suicidal depression. He had a girlfriend, but the relationship ended badly. Soothing himself with *American Bandstand* and the greatest hits of James Baldwin, Norman Mailer, and William Burroughs, songs and books were the perfect match for his mind, burning with questions of death, yet brightened by the sensation of being wholly alive. Taking up the restorative art of painting, his figures were unusually grotesque, the self-portraits and off-color scribblings were of a person disturbed. Heading to Florida, to live with his grandparents and attend St. Petersburg Junior College, he wasted no time seeking out the town's one and only burlesque show and making friends at the coffeehouses. He saw his first foreign film, Godard's *Une femme est une femme*. It was his introduction to the new wave of French cinema.

"I'm interested in film because to me I believe it's the closest approximation in art that we have to the actual flow of consciousness, in both dream life, and in the everyday perception of the world," he said.

He discovered open mic nights, performing his Beat recitations, to the accompaniment of his own ukulele strums. He felt most at home in verse and hoped to get better at reading, though as a poet, he said he felt naked and inept. But as a showman, Jim was already polishing his act: public urination was a specialty, and he'd logged his first arrest, for toying with a policeman's hat. He'd found trouble at the coffeehouse too – something sexual, quite possibly scandalous by local standards – and the regulars thought he'd do well to move on, though leaving was complicated. He'd met his sweetheart on the beach in Clearwater. Jim and Mary Werbelow were in love, though he'd leave her in summer – the Indian summer – to study theater arts, in Tallahassee.

Hitchhiking 200 miles on a lonesome stretch of highway, weekends were spent on the road to Mary in Tampa Bay. Painting his dreams in notebooks, the highway became a canvas to chart ideas, and note phrases, variations on his night theme; hidden in notebooks, always notebooks, carried at all times, even all the way out West, the place it was determined was best – for a person like Jim.

And when he arrived – to the Golden State where *Eureka!* they'd found it, and it found him – he followed the poet Arthur Rimbaud's directive, to disorder the senses, and make his soul monstrous. Becoming a poet for the multitudes, a prophet of their end times from his outpost in Los Angeles, he became a shadow as long as the days were excruciatingly bright, in the city of angels, the city of night, the place where he is, was, and always shall be, Jim Morrison.

Addressing the unpredictability of power and war, our fair sister earth and her daughters, he asked his listeners to live fearlessly and free. The lone vagrant and trickster, the romantic troubadour, Dionysus, drunken maniac, clean shaven, bearded, suited in leather and denim, in buckskin, in snakeskin, in his own skin and no shirt at all, the erotic politician, the wild child, and the Lizard King, let his mojo rise until it became the soundtrack to a lifetime, or two or three. His theatrics roused suspicions, his words made men irate; but these were not just his words; rather, they belonged to the ages, a prophetic light on the edge of darkness. Appealing to both boys and girls, lost in the world, searching for their own gold, he harnessed the collective moan, gave it a voice and unleashed it:

Blood on the streets it's up to my ankles
We want the world and we want it now
This is the end, beautiful friend, the end

His words really meant something then; 50 years later, they still do.

CHAPTER 1
This is The End: 1964-1965

Jim Morrison got into town just in time to spend Christmas with his family on Coronado, a small strip of land off the California coast near San Diego. For twenty years, the Morrison family had remained in motion, moving from town to town, and grown accustomed to being packed up and shipped off to other vistas on order of its pater familias. But the move at the end of 1963 was different: its initiation was Jim's.

Observing his interests, and knowing Florida State University would limit a young man like him, college friends were first to suggest he move West. Thanks to his family residing in-state, Jim could better pursue his interests in French cinema and symbolist poetry and receive a top-flight education at a state school tuition rate at the University of California, Los Angeles (UCLA). The plan was for his girlfriend Mary Werbelow to join him there, though until then, the end of the year family holiday would serve as a final farewell, signaling Jim's Southern California future without them. Few could've predicted that this otherwise ordinary Christmas scene would lead in a couple of years to the development of a monstrous personality, dominating and disrupting rock' n' roll on stages from the East Coast to the West.

Perhaps it was only natural coming of age in the '60s, the son of a naval man, in possession of a prankster's wit and a taste for underground culture, would light out to create his own story with a dark narrative. Certainly his words to "The End" would allude to the beginnings of the dystopian dream. But in California, the visions and weird scenes, formed inside UCLA's grand halls and bungalow classrooms, or while peeping out a window from the back of the blue bus, would begin to billow and unfold, as if written on the Santa Ana winds with Jim's name on them. Insisting he was a person of unknown origins, intent on bringing back the ancient rituals of paganism, a 20-year-old Morrison searched his dreams and began to chase them, blowing through a fresh season of hell in Los Angeles.

Portrait of the Artist

Enrolling as a junior in January of 1964, Morrison would be completing UCLA's four-year film program in just two years. "The entire history of film is only about 60 years old ... Anybody can be an expert. I love that about it,"[1] he once told fellow student Ray Manzarek. Based on their creative output and outside interests, both Manzarek and Morrison would develop reputations on campus as rulebreakers. Ray was Jim's elder by four years— a graduate student pursuing a master's in film following his economics degree and a stint in the army; he was happily in a relationship with Dorothy Fujikawa, a fellow art student who would soon become his wife. Morrison was seeing Mary, who had just arrived from Florida, and Manzarek remembered her as a girl everyone loved, especially Jim. "She was Jim's first love. She held a deep place in his soul,"[2] he said.

At UCLA, Morrison would view the world through a filter of friends and film history, while sharpening the tools that would bring to life his jotted phrases, pornographic cartoons, and anti-establishment themes he'd been scrawling in his notebooks for years. He developed his ideas and increased his explorations in classes on human behavior and psychology, as well as in theater. Rooted in a passion, attraction, and nostalgia for the State of California, the Western Spirit, and its mythic yet palpable legacy, the formal education and a personal affection for Indian myths, French movies, Greek mythology, German philosophy, Beat and surrealist poetry, and music—from the Blues to *Howl*—gelled into Jim's own brand of pioneering California cosmology.

Bruin Life

Opening in the building that today houses the LA Central Library, and following a move to Vermont Avenue (now LA City College), in 1927, UCLA made Westwood its home. Officially addressed 405 Hilgard, and bordered by Le Conte, Gayley, Veteran and Sunset Boulevard, UCLA, known largely for its Greek life, football, and college spirit, was the second campus, following Berkeley, to be established in the University of California system. With enrollment at around 30,000, UCLA was generally the largest of the 10 universities, running neck and neck with

Cal Berkeley as the state's most prestigious, contributing toward a notorious rivalry between the campuses. There was a time when UC was considered among the best public university systems in the world.

Morrison's induction as a California student artist of the '60s coincided with the period during which Americans were still mourning the loss of their President—in the window after the November Kennedy assassination, but before the February arrival of the Beatles and a new era. Beat culture and the nascent hippie movement were already established, while religious and spiritual experimentation all flowered, stirring a climate in seemingly perfect harmony with the ideas Jim was cultivating and hoping to manifest. Political and social engagement swirled in the air as free speech, anti-war, and environmental advocates organized. In California, black, brown, and white were not mandated by the state to segregate, and student leaders and organizers of all races were emerging. On the surface, California may've seemed more tolerant to alternative points of views and lifestyles and compared to the southern United States, relative racial harmony existed. But J. Edgar Hoover's FBI were also on the scene, monitoring the student activity, disapproving, and ultimately disempowering it.

By the time Morrison dropped in on campus and its nearby beach towns, drugs—natural and chemical varieties—were in peak circulation, and in wide use for recreational, medical, and religious experimentation. Though thousands like him migrated to the state in the '60s to take advantage of its rugged landscape and freedom culture, California was more than just a wild and free place for Jim: It was a sacred space, where he was at his most peaceful tapping into the energy of the earth. From its gentle redwood giants to its prehistoric cacti, California's landscape still had patches that were untrammeled, though its ancient peoples had largely vanished from the land, banished to folktales and California Mission pictorials. Morrison's writings conveyed a natural empathy, if not a kinship, with its indigenous people. As players in his distinctly western dreams and visions, Morrison's connection to the ancestral residents as well as his concern for future generations, gave them roles in a new kind of drama, a sort of apocalyptic western movie, developing in his mind. Existing as ghosts, their souls hovered over the state's bright morning light and dark coastal nights, their stories and cautionary tales of a future waiting to be told.

The California campus was also Morrison's gateway to greater LA, his beloved city of night. From his residence in student housing at UCLA Co-Op, he accessed every aspect of what the state had to offer, from sand, surf, and mountain canyons to the west, to the downtown urban center and desert further east. The combination of influences altered and informed his work, consciously and subconsciously, quickly revealing his promise as an iconoclastic artist of the West. A six-hour drive north would land him in the Bay Area, the western outpost of innovation, creativity and freethinking; to the south was Mexico, a further source of uncharted mystery for him. The 20-minute ride by Big Blue Bus to Venice Beach, with its palm trees, fine sand, glassy Santa Monica Bay, and lineaments of shore life were familiar to him from his time in Tampa Bay, all of it fuel for a beach person like Jim.

With most of his nights in the Deep South devoted to traveling back and forth on the road to Mary, Jim had grown comfortable with being alone, in darkened rooms and on lonesome stretches of highway. In Westwood Village, the nexus of campus life, Morrison was most drawn to its multiple cinemas, where he was free to dream, for hours or days, while the movies provided an education and an escape for him. The depth and breadth of film history, and its connection to surrealism, would soon be revealed through his studies, but Hollywood history had already left its mark on him: Nicolas Ray's *Rebel Without A Cause*, was the genesis of his developing love of cinema. The very spot at Griffith Park Observatory where James Dean had performed in character as Jimbo had left an indelible impression on a 15-year-old Jim: now just a short ride away from the location, pilgrimage visitations would follow.

High on life and art, he embarked on a series of examinations and discoveries that took him from higher consciousness to the lower depths. There was little room for anything quotidian: Looking like an average All-American with a hint of Beat tucked inside his mind, Jim was wide open to big ideas, quick to catch on to them, and it was a fact: UCLA's rigorous film arts program offered a sea of possibility well beyond what he had known on the Gulf Coast and the occasional art house screening. Captivated by the language of film, an art he could imprint with his poet's sensibilities, he preferred the fringe over Tinsel Town styles, and dug into the experimental modes of the underground—the New American Cinema forged by Bruce Connor, Jonas Mekas, Stan Brakhage, and

Kenneth Anger–early '60s filmmakers informed largely by the European avant-garde movement of the 1920s.

Movies, Marlene and Artaud

During their years at the UCLA film studies program, both Morrison and Manzarek took the courses taught by Josef Von Sternberg, maker of *The Blue Angel* (*Der Blau Angel*), and other films starring Marlene Dietrich. Von Sternberg had landed at UCLA following the Hollywood portion of his career, the consummation of his collaboration with Dietrich on six pictures, including *The Devil is a Woman*, a favorite of Morrison's. The director had come from the silent era's German school of filmmakers who emphasized *mise en scene*, or the design aspects of production, and he carried over that aesthetic into his talkies with Dietrich, making them visually distinct. Von Sternberg's career in film was largely complete when he taught classes from 1959-1963 in the film school's bungalows, but Manzarek suggested in his memoirs that the professor/director was perhaps the greatest of all influences on his band's work. "I know he had a profound effect on the Doors' music," wrote Manzarek. "A music that was slightly kinky and slightly Germanic."[3] Indeed, remnants of German philosophy and Weimar culture would be heard in the Doors' compositions, but Von Sternberg's film inventions, a touchstone for its dramatic arc, staging, and production values, can also be traced as influential to the band's general presentation. In addition to film theory and history, Morrison learned film practice, running sound, and cameras in his classes and workshops, as in his Saturday session, Theater Arts 170, with its emphasis on *cinéma vérité*.

Had Manzarek and Morrison attended the film program at UCLA just a bit earlier than they did, they would've sat in on lectures by Jean Renoir, director of French cinema classics, *The Grand Illusion* and *Rules of the Game;* as it was, they became self-educated experts in contemporary French films, *La Nouvelle Vague,* that produced Jean Luc Goddard and François Truffaut. *Contempt* (*Le Mépris*) and *Band of Outsiders* (*Bande à part*), *The 400 Blows* (*Les Quatre Cents Coup*) and *Jules et Jim* were all making the rounds of American art houses at the time. He discovered less celebrated but equally influential filmmakers, Jean-Pierre Melville, Éric Rohmer, and Agnès Varda, but it was Godard's style that most immediately connected with Morrison who hadn't easily forgotten the 1961 picture, *A Woman is a Woman (Une Femme est une femme),* his first brush with a foreign film. In seeking to create a kind of epic cinema, in which the viewer becomes alienated or distanced from the action, Godard took his cues from German dramatist, Bertolt Brecht, whose work had also begun to seep into the consciousness of the UCLA film school set.

Brecht, Weill and Lotte Lenya

Bertolt Brecht's productions– highlighting where morality and humanity truly vied and shook up existing, stock notions of choice and values, song craft and content—were an early source of inspiration for both Morrison and Manzarek. Upon his flight from Germany, Bertolt Brecht had moved to the West Coast in the World War II years. He

settled in Santa Monica in the early 1940s, attempting to secure writing work in Hollywood (he found some on Fritz Lang's *The Hangmen Also Die*). He was also among those famously targeted in the US by Senator Joseph McCarthy as were his politically engaged Hollywood brethren during the town's blacklist era. Called to testify in front of the House UnAmerican Activities Committee (HUAC) in 1947, he returned to East Germany, where he lived until his death in 1956. His Santa Monica home, at 1063 26th Street, is designated a historical landmark.

Brecht's writing partner Kurt Weill and his wife Lotte Lenya, the singer and actress best known for performing his songs, also fled Germany during the rise of the Third Reich, the period in which the Brecht/Weill songbook was largely banned from performance. Lenya went on to win a Tony award for her portrait of Pirate Jenny in *The Threepenny Opera* in New York. Becoming a fixture on the theater and cabaret scene and in student record collections, Lenya remained in New York following Weill's death until her own in 1981. One of her best known performances, "Alabama Song," from *The Rise and Fall of the City of Mahoganny*, is an effective discombobulation that captures conflicting energies: The sound of the tune, combined with the action on the stage and the upbeat nature of the lyric, forces the listener to wonder, "What exactly is going on here?" It

> is at once haunting and alienating, forceful and upending—much like Morrison and Manzarek's own music would one day become. The pair would go on to replicate Brecht's confrontational, epic theater, which attempted to critique ancient as well as modern institutions, from the church to capitalism.

Morrison, Manzarek, and Dorothy Fujikawa sought out all the most experimental, underground and talked about theater arts programs and film screenings in town. During a semester break, on a weekend in Berkeley, the couple ran into Morrison at a cinema showing Jean Genet's *Un Chant D'amour*. A discourse on race, class, and freedom, seeped in homoerotic imagery, *Un Chant D'amour* is a prison story in which the power of imagination triumphs over the powers that be. "I kinda thought you'd be here,"[4] Dorothy said to Jim after the screening.

Back at UCLA, Morrison was also studying French surrealism with the poet and translator Jack Hirschman. Teaching the works of Paul Éluard, Max Jacob, Pierre Reverdy, Raymond Queneau, and especially actor, playwright, and director, Antonin Artaud, Professor Hirschman's *Artaud Anthology* was published by City Lights Books in 1965, and contributed toward a greater understanding of the artist among his fellows and scholars. (Hirschman went on to become the poet laureate of San Francisco and recognized around the world as a revolutionary poet; his time at UCLA ended abruptly, when it was discovered he was encouraging and assisting students in resisting the Vietnam War). Artaud launched his most significant work in theater in the early part of the 20th Century in France: he wrote the German expressionist film directed by Germaine Dulac, *The Seashell and the Clergyman,* on which Salvador Dali and Luis Buñuel based *Un Chien Andalou.* Artaud's manifesto for a Theater of Cruelty was published in 1931; his best known work, *The Theater and its Double* was published in 1938 and contained both manifestos on the theater of cruelty—advocating for blood curdling screams and other primal sounds of expression, as well as theatrical devices, like extreme lighting. Artaud's experiments with peyote in Mexico and his addiction to opium, prescribed for other ailments, found him alternately misdiagnosed and institutionalized. Though he endured a psychotic break, his theatrical experiments were impassioned, intellectual efforts based on the ancient and Eastern cultural forms he deeply revered.

Believing western production values were in the process of killing theater traditions, Artaud attempted to pinpoint a concept of Life as Art. Emerging as the Theater of Cruelty, an attempt to overthrow forms and create a kind of chaotic effect, the approach, along with Artaud's drug experiences, significantly drove Morrison's relationship to the power of his own landscape, at the edge of the world in the American West. Artaud's vision, that an audience should receive the maximum impact from the theater-going experience, was the big idea for Morrison and it would not let him rest. His studious determination resulted in a devotion to making art, and reflected an often extreme and difficult life.

"The more abusive you are, the more they love it," said Morrison in later years, and it seems he believed it.

"You've got to believe you're doing them a favor by being on stage."⁵

Rimbaud

If there is one poet with whom Morrison is most often allied, it is Arthur Rimbaud (1854-1891), the French teenaged rebel whose tenure pre-figured surrealism and whose life had a number of curious parallels with Morrison's own. As a military son, and a defiant one, he was a vagabond who willfully chose to roam. He was of this world, and yet his perceptions of things beyond it – of the eternal –were so deeply etched, they would inform artists, musicians, and poets for ages to come. Living roughly and suffering for art contributed toward his desired "derangement of the senses," which he believed would help a man better know his own soul. Inspired as he was by the writings of François-René de Chateaubriand and Victor Hugo, Théodore de Banville and Charles Baudelaire, Rimbaud wrote of the sea and the land, and the solitary men who explored the wilderness. "La Bateau ivre" (*"The Drunken Boat"*) written when the poet was just 16, details his willingness to live an unconventional life for art's sake. "I was indifferent to all crews...The Rivers let me go where I wanted...*Le Flueves m'ont laissé descendre où je voulais."*

In 1966, translator Wallace Fowlie published *Rimbaud: Complete Works, Selected Letters*. In correspondence to Fowlie from Morrison in 1968, the singer explained he had a habit of carrying the book with him at all times. In addition to the plain English translation, Morrison appreciated the cover, a drawing by Picasso of the poet as a scruffy young man. So inspired, Morrison began to develop his own uncommon language and sense of wild and restless symbolism that characterized his own surrealistic oeuvre, while presenting himself as similarly unkempt.

Rimbaud's works, especially the 1871 poem "La Bateau ivre" and the full length, *Une Saison en enfer* (*A Season In Hell*), have remained influential to poets and artists, particularly those working on the fringes and in extremes. In his revolutionary use of symbolism depicting the challenges of creating art and poetry, Rimbaud's spirit continued to rise in the form of Beat literature and later in punk rock lyrics, but most pervasively in the transcendent highs and low-rent lows reflected in the poems and songs of Jim Morrison.

"This phenomenon of Rimbaud's appeal to the rock music world is not easy to explain or analyze, but I believe it will have to be assessed and explored in any future study of spirituality in today's world,"[6] wrote Fowlie in his 1994 memoir, *Rimbaud and Jim Morrison*. Certainly Rimbaud's appeal to rock musicians has maintained, as has listener devotion to the freedom call of rock music and the musicians who play it in its purest form. Though it is safe to say that in the modern world, the cult of celebrity has largely replaced non-materialist values like artistic and personal freedom set forth in the work of Rimbaud, Jim Morrison, and others like them. Rock 'n' roll's incarnation in contemporary consumer-driven culture demonstrates a public's willingness to worship the idea of freedom in the abstract, while its creators largely remain chained to the conventions their libertine heroes and heroines railed against.

Culture of the Times

Throughout the '60s, popular music, movies, and the literary arts increasingly reflected the energy of a youth culture on the road to enlightenment, as an entire generation mobilized around matters of civil rights, free speech, and being against the war in Vietnam. Fuelled by books, films, the idealism of youth, and the influence of alternative and ancient philosophies, Morrison and his artistic peers were swept up by the energetic wave of cultural upheaval and rising consciousness, while under the influence of the artistic and literary movements preceding them. He formed unique perspectives as an artist, taking notes, reading, writing, engaging in discussion, and filling his well against the backdrop of an unpopular overseas war—a war with which his father was directly involved.

In 1964, Jim's father, Admiral Steve Morrison, commanded the forces in the Gulf of Tonkin: the battle at sea opened the door to further invasion by US forces on the ground in Southeast Asia and combat in North Vietnam.

Jim grew further fascinated with the corollaries between the "psychic purge" that produced the creative energy of Germany's post World War I Weimar culture and the energy produced by the '60s rock 'n' roll counterculture in the United States. Whether the onstage experiments of Bertolt Brecht and Antonin Artaud, the visions of William Blake, or the romantic rebellions of Arthur Rimbaud, he drew inspiration from European history, from prophetic poetry and from the political potential of classical to experimental theater. Studying its rise and reflecting on its inevitable fall, Jim Morrison had learned to make room for historic precedent in his own inquiries into contemporary Western civilization.

Graduation

Controversy surrounded Morrison and Manzarek's culminating film school projects. Morrison's student film vaguely concerned a melee following a stag film breaking mid-reel; it starred a lingerie-clad girl bumping and grinding atop a TV console as a reel of old World War II film clips unspooled, bombs bursting in air. Unfortunately, in a situation of life imitating art, Jim's poorly rendered edits caught in the projector, abruptly ending the film department's prestigious screening event at Royce Hall on the UCLA campus.

Manzarek's student films were chosen to screen in 1964 and 1965. Though he'd been advised to remove a shower scene from *Evergreen*, his film featuring his girlfriend, Dorothy Fujikawa, he chose not to comply with the conservative film regents' request, then caught hell from professors after the show. But the screening of an uncut *Evergreen* would prove to be a mini-watershed: not only did its people (Bertolt Brecht) and places (the Whisky) foreshadow things in what would become part of the Doors' own history, it demonstrated the changing of the guard on campuses across the nation. Power was being transferred from administrators to a restless student body, determined to upset the balance and put it into the hands of the people.

While two men's artistic merits certainly weren't going to change the world, a series of them, across campuses, in coffeehouses, throughout the nation, signaled a cultural shift: Counterculture revolution seemed a possibility. What Morrison and Manzarek witnessed and gained in their campus years were not only an education and instruction in the arts, but tangible proof, through energetic study and execution, that art - even their own student films - could elicit feverish responses and emotions, and raise awareness toward positive action and increased freedom of expression: Art at its best could make a statement and a difference.

Though his earliest attempts at disruption were awkward and poorly rendered, Jim's contribution was rousing nonetheless, yet he was temporarily chastened by his bad luck streak at the film school screenings. As Mary Werbelow remembered it, "You're going to leave me," he said to her, shortly after delivering the news of his artistic failing. Mary did leave him soon after the event, but not for any lack of confidence in Jim as an artist. When she caught him with another woman, their romance effectively came to an end, though their relationship took on another shape and significance. As for UCLA's Royce Hall, by the 21st Century it was hosting one of Southern California's most adventurously programmed performing arts calendars. But UCLA's radical student and professorial past has largely been expunged from its history and the school has become the scene of much anti-diversity and anti-affirmative action campaigning – a curious outcome for a campus that gestated the '60s uprising, from initiating minority studies departments, to fostering poets, musicians, and cultural agitators like Jim Morrison.

Maintaining his interest in film as the years went by, Morrison dreamed, "I'd like to write and direct a film of my own." Unable to foresee a future for himself as a film scholar or in a technical or creative role like cinematographer or director, he set his sights on heading east to New York where he hoped to fall in with Jonas Mekas and his experimental film cooperative. "The Mekas Brothers are no longer the gentle poets that they thought they were; they are two wild Indians drying scalps," wrote *Cahiers du Cinema* of their 1964 film, *The Brig*. Practicing an extreme, avant garde approach to cinema, it was the exact kind of scene that appealed to Jim as he prepared to leave school with a head full of book knowledge but few prospects beyond his intent to marry his skills, aesthetics, and creative mind to living as an artist.

Prepared to go without immediate material gratification, he claimed not to mind what some perceived as struggle as long as his lack of luxury afforded him the kind of freedom money could not buy. Like the philosophers, writers, and spiritualists of the early 20th Century who inspired him, he would make art from life. Bidding farewell to Ray, Dorothy, and Mary Werbelow, and preparing to leave that which was known to him at UCLA, in 1965 he received his undergraduate degree from UCLA, a B.S. in cinematography, from the Theatre Arts Department of the College of Fine Arts. Uninterested in attending the commencement ceremony where he'd claim his diploma, he asked it be sent to his parents' address.

But Jim never actually made it to New York that summer. Magnetized by the energy of Venice Beach, his passion for symbolist poetry and the feelings of possibility viewed from California's coast, those key elements combined to make a new kind of West Coast artistry, and developed into a voice his own.

CHAPTER 2
Santa Monica, Venice, and The Doors of Perception: 1965-1966

Conducting his own post-graduate studies in human behavior and the nature of good and evil, Morrison took it upon himself to become further acquainted with Frederich Nietzsche, the German philosopher who'd wielded a heavy influence on one of his literary heroes, Jack Kerouac. Adopting ideas suggesting how to move beyond the repression that certain moral codes dictated, Morrison began to reject conventional doctrines and wrest a meaning of life from nihilist philosophy and other writings on morality, while also studying William Blake's illuminations and poetry as prophesy.

With the intention to rouse the spirit and awaken society from its collective slumber, writing poetry had overtaken filmmaking as Morrison's potential life direction. Creating his own images with words, juxtaposing disturbing ideas with often-violent rhetoric, he began to perceive the work of artists and poets as one of great responsibility. He reasoned that taking a radical stand through statement and action could save the world from its own destruction, and he had not come to this notion by chance, nor was it as far-fetched or pie-in-the-sky as it might sound.

Within the '60s counterculture, and even the culture at large, there was once a wide swath of believers in the idea of the artist and thinker's job, as one whose work was to not only create and foster beauty and civility, but to conceptualize the future and explore the unknown. Commercial gain and engagement were secondary to aesthetic, artistic, and humanistic concerns. But only a true seer could recognize the seriousness of such a prospect – devoting one's self to seeing the big picture and reporting back is arduous work. Whether conceiving of improvements to society, challenging the status quo, or simply recording what he saw, Morrison, bantering among peers, filmmaking friends, and the artists of Venice, was developing a symbolist poetry. He also made time for a growing collection of less-directed companions: hustlers and schemers, drug dealers and drinkers, partners in crime and punishing addictions, who provided him with experience and street wisdom, while he stoked the fire of his own alcoholism. Morrison may or may not yet have been entirely up to the serious artist's task, but he was certainly armed with information and a passion to deliver: With his borrowed set of art school ideas, he set about deranging and disassembling himself in an effort to make the world more beautiful and whole.

Though the world-famous Acid Tests in Northern California had yet to be conducted, in the summer of 1965, Morrison and Manzarek had already experimented with the psychedelic drug, liking its effects. Morrison especially spent the season soaking in a combined mix of LSD, beer, and other substances. Surviving on very little food and plenty of drugs, he dropped 30 pounds in an incredibly short period of time and became a truly starving poet. Spending the beach season shuffling around Venice and its environs, he surfed from couch to couch and legendarily slept under the eaves of the Santa Monica Pier. Alternately stargazing, smoking, drinking, and writing, he eventually landed on the roof of 14 Westminster Avenue, the apartment of Dennis Jakob, a friend from film school.

With no limitations or filters on him, no one giving him feedback on his art or his imagination, Jim's time in his makeshift rooftop bedroom was a chance to collect solitary time, experience a slip into unconsciousness, and explore a creative space previously unknown to him; it was in essence, a kind of apprenticeship in shamanism. The western edge of the continent was his cocoon while he was becoming Jim Morrison: singer, seer, and man of vision and sorrow.

Venice of the West

Originally conceived as a resort town in the early 1900s, Venice's main street is named for Abbot Kinney, a developer with a vision of his own sort: He aimed to turn what was essentially marshland into something more spectacular, a Venice of the West. Installing a miniature railway, a gondola system, and an amusement pier, Venice was successful for a time at drawing tourists. But following Kinney's death, the town ultimately

couldn't sustain itself and by 1925, Los Angeles had annexed it. By the time Charlie Chaplin set up shop there in the early Hollywood era, it was becoming an artist enclave. In 1958, Venice's Windward Avenue, with its storefront structures resembling Tijuana, was used as the setting for the Orson Welles film *A Touch of Evil*, adding to the locale's allure and mystique. The film noir starring Janet Leigh and Charlton Heston features remnants of the beach town's Venetian architecture, most visible in the film's opening sequence. Increasingly neglected and falling into disrepair in the '50s, Venice began attracting artists and immigrants to its cheap bungalows and coffeehouse/galleries, like the Gas House and Venice West, established during the '50s Beat era. Poets and visual artists were drawn to the town's dusty and dilapidated shores: Wallace Berman and his circle of artist and actor friends associated with the Ferus Gallery, were all part of this Venice axis. Poets Philomene Long, Tony Scibella, Stuart Perkoff, Frank Rios, Will Margolis, Aya, and John Thomas are among the poets from the area, along with visual artists Ed Kienholz, Ed Moses, and Ed Ruscha. "If you think of America as a large table cloth and you hold it up and shake it, all the debris comes down to Venice," says Philomene Long. "In Venice is the residue of the freest country in the world." Frank Rios adds, "If you own nothing, you have nothing to lose and you're free."[1]

Where Venice Meets Turkey Joint West

Call it dark blues rock with a West Coast psychedelic consciousness: A new style of music was being born during that "Beautiful hot summer," as Morrison remembered it, "And I just started hearing songs." Pulling lines together from fragments of poems and phrases scribbled in his notebook – the one his friends say he was in the habit of carrying with him, ever since Florida – the verses were informed by a reading list so sophisticated and vast, the average rock fan and critic would blanche. And yet, these shards of smart and surreal phrases were perfect for a new breed of otherworldly rock song that was circulating in the mid '60s, fuelled by drugs and in Morrison's case, poetics.

Let's swim to the moon
Let's climb through the tide
Surrender to the waiting worlds
That lap against our side

The songs contained visions not necessarily of loveliness but reckoned with emotion – from elation to despair – as real to him as the phases of the moon or the turning of the tide on a moonlight drive.

"Those first five or six rock songs I wrote, I was just taking notes at a fantastic rock concert inside my head," he said. "And once I had written the songs, I had to sing them,"[2]. Morrison remembered in a *Rolling Stone* interview with Jerry Hopkins.

Young artists Ray Manzarek and Dorothy Fujikawa were naturally drawn to the Venice area and lived in Santa Monica's bordering Ocean Park district. With Dorothy at work as a tape cleaner, Ray found the days long, with plenty of time to practice his new habit of meditation on the sand. In his own words he was "being a bum," though he still had a gig with his blues band, Rick and the Ravens (featuring brothers Rick and Jim Manczarek, as Manzarek was originally spelled) at Santa Monica's Turkey Joint West. On the corner of Second Street and Santa Monica Boulevard (and since converted to an English pub, Ye Old Kings Head), the place would pack out with college students and beach locals. In contrast to Venice's literary and arts scene, Rick and the Ravens' music was less original and more standard – bar band music – far removed from the authentic blues or original rock evolving in California at the time. There was a time that a beer-soaked Jim Morrison stopped by Turkey Joint West for a couple of drunken rounds of "Louie Louie": Early in his tenure at UCLA, it was his first stint as a singer with a band, but it wasn't much of a performance, and Jim wasn't much of a singer then, though he enjoyed the spotlight, especially with a couple of drinks in him.

But playing accompaniment to the adolescent action in a college bar was not the kind of life Manzarek had envisioned for himself. As he lay on the beach, recovering from a gig, he began to meditate when seemingly out of nowhere, Jim appeared beside him on the sand. So goes the legend of how the Doors were formed, but the roots of the meeting are in reality. It had been months since they'd seen each other and as they caught up, Jim said he'd been writing. Ray persuaded him to recite the verses of "Moonlight Drive," "My Eyes Have Seen You," and "Summer's Almost Gone," his edge-of-the-world West Coast symphonies. As their road map to the future began to unfurl on the stretch of beach between Venice and Santa Monica Pier, Ray told Jim he could stay with him and Dorothy at their garage apartment on the Venice border. Forsaking their own bed for him at 147 Fraser Street, in Santa Monica, Jim moved in and escaped the daytime madness of drinking and drugging and nights spent homeless and alone in Venice. He even had a nightstand, on which to rest his paperbacks of *Ulysses* by James Joyce, *A Season in Hell* by Rimbaud, and Céline's *Journey to the End of the Night*.

Imagining the possibilities, pondering what lay beyond the horizon, far-off in the distance, the future was uncertain, on that they could agree (though something told both Morrison and Manzarek that China held the keys to it). From the series of endless nights, daydreaming and soul-mining, an interior mood music was developing based on Morrison's words to the summer-lit "Moonlight Drive," "Summer's Almost Gone," and "Indian Summer." The songs were springing to life from the free space devoted to a combination of reading, writing, and downtime during which the trio lived a good life on a tight budget. Dorothy's paycheck provided the essentials; their fare was supplemented with items liberated by Jim from the aisles of the supermarket on Lincoln and Ocean Park. Ray spearheaded their fitness regime and added a beach workout on their walks from the apartment, north to the Pier. Pausing at the old Muscle Beach for a go on the rungs of the monkey bars, the sand served as a muse and inspiration for musicians in training: The daily exercise added discipline and structure to the days, along with some necessary bulk to their weak and slight frames.

Muscle Beach

The idea that artists (and all workers) need a limber body in alignment with mind and spirit is a well conceived and acknowledged notion (if not necessarily widely practiced). As a commission of the 1930s Works Progress Administration (WPA), Muscle Beach was just one of the many building and arts projects providing jobs to millions in a time of economic crisis; the WPA created a lasting legacy of improved civic infrastructure and healthier societal conditions. In the case of Muscle Beach, the public installation of gymnastics and workout equipment directly contributed to the birth of the physical fitness movement of the mid-20th Century.

The original generation of bodybuilders, including Jack LaLanne and Steve Reeves, were said to have gotten their start on the beach's parallel bars and gymnastic rings, while acrobats and gymnasts also used the area to sharpen their acts (a jungle gym and swing set remains). In 1959, a sex crime involving the bodybuilders who congregated there led to a dismantling of the site by Santa Monica authorities: All bodybuilding activity moved down the beach to Venice, where there remains a community of fitness and weight-training devotees. By the '90s, acrobats had

returned to Santa Monica's old workout spot and today, there exists two stretches of Muscle Beach, within walking distance of each other. Anyone in search of the vista from Morrison and Manzarek's perspective should head in the direction of Santa Monica, home of the Original Muscle Beach (denoted by a marker), while those looking for competitive muscle-flexing will find it in Venice. Body alteration, modification, and perfection through exercise, nutrition, and supplements were born on LA beaches: it's a culture that continues to thrive in this far western outpost of body building and fitness.

Committed to becoming stronger physically, Morrison and Manzarek developed new muscles creatively and spiritually (Manzarek through meditation and Morrison through philosophical tenets, while both experimented chemically). Working on their strength, they worked on their songs, and then they worked some more. Riding across the Westside to UCLA, they helped themselves to a piano in the music department practice rooms, and their songs began to take shape. Getting up and walking on the beach, working out, writing, and doing it again, they eventually started swinging from bar to bar, on the workout equipment, as well as in their songs and phrases.

The highway at the "End of the Night," borrowed its title from Céline, and its verse from William Blake: *Some are born to sweet delight, some are born to endless night.* The similarly eerie "Summer's Almost Gone," is dipped in psychedelic bluesology, as are the more frantic "My

Eyes Have Seen You," and the primitive boogie-woogie number, "Go Insane." The slip and slide of "Moonlight Drive," and the upbeat but descending melody of "Hello I Love You" shared similar qualities: Moody, simple, and haunting, they were spiked with mystery, and strangely unique.

Beyond the sun and surf in the Bay Cities, a gloomy daytime haze and foggy evenings characterize California summer coastal conditions. In the chill of the night Ray and Dorothy had each other to hold; Jim stayed warm in the bleak and damp cold with the electric blanket he was attached to using. Grappling with the loss of the love of Mary Werbelow, he remembered the warmth of their shared sunsets over the Gulf of Mexico, from the water's edge in Clearwater and St. Petersburg on Indian Rock Beach, the land of the Seminole. Every footprint on Western sand – from Ocean Park to the Pier, surrounded by teenagers, flirting and sunbathing from sun-up to sundown – became fuel for his songs. Immersed in memory material, he could become the lone vagrant, the highwayman and vagabond, and set off to explore Chumash territory and the California night, with no guru or shaman to guide him.

California Soul

As a Far West mecca for searchers of all types, Los Angeles would become the base of operations for all varieties of spiritual, New Age, and people-powered movements. Inhabited by a class of seekers and a populace seemingly more in need of a spiritual refreshment than anywhere else on earth, there is something about the desert landscape, personal temperament, and presence of tremendous wealth that draws serious-minded seekers as well as dabblers toward the myriad of alternative beliefs, treatments, remedies, curatives, palliatives, and placebos available for sale and for free, statewide.

Following the Mexican-American War, when California was ceded to the US in 1848, Los Angeles was largely grazing land for cattle, feeding hungry miners during the gold rush. But once fortunes began to dwindle, and vigilantes and lynch mobs ran out anyone who wasn't wanted from San Francisco, LA became a kind of lawless place. The seekers who rushed to the state in 1849 had by 1855 totaled a population of about 300,000 from all different parts of the world – immigrants (especially from China and Italy) seeking the proverbial better life for their families. But the influx of population and emphasis on personal gain came at a great cost to the environment and its indigenous people, who according to carbon dating had inhabited the land since about 2600 B.C. The gold rush not only negatively impacted the landscape, but the Indian population was nearly wiped out by forms of disease thriving among prospectors, diseases previously unknown to them.

What have they done to the earth?
What have they done to our fair sister?

Morrison calling upon the spirits – the Indians who occupied the highways of his mind, marshalling the available forces to overcome the powers of evil – was working in the tradition of efforts of early 20th Century psychologist and philosopher William James whose mind-world connections served as a template for the avant garde in art and literature. The Spiritualists of the late 19th and early 20th Centuries – their work a response to women's suffrage, slavery, and the massive casualties of war – were the forerunners of this new age in thought that merged native American ritual with the occult, Christian mysticism, and neo-paganism. By the 1930s, an influx of Eastern spirituality had taken hold in California and started to make its way around the world. By mid-century, a new brand of distinctly California consciousness had evolved to pick up the threads of the transcendentalist movement of 19th century literary America. East Indian met Indigenous American, met Jew, met Morman, met Catholic, met pagan ritualist. A vortex for spiritual seekers and awareness, California was the place where German philosophic reasoning and psychology, crisscrossed with Vedanta, its practice derived from Sanskrit texts; devotees of various faiths co-mingled in perfect harmony, though diabolical death cults also came to call California home. Incidentally, Clearwater Florida, where Morrison had lived with his grandparents, is the headquarters of the Church of Scientology, the religion with allusions to aliens and extraterrestrials, founded by science fiction author, L. Ron Hubbard. Scientology also has an extremely strong base in Los Angeles, where it established itself in 1954.

The circumstances informing previous movements to end suffering were not unlike the worldwide conditions that provoked an awakening and surge of interest in manifesting new realities from California in the '60s when religious sciences, the California desert, and the wild west coast converged and birthed a new frontier of thought. Ultimately dubbed the new age movement, even the state's government had its transcendental side. Environmental protection ideas developed early in the decade during the term of Governor Pat Brown, and put California at the forefront of environmental preservation versus natural resources debates. In later years, from 1975-1983, Brown's son, Jerry, who'd once studied for the priesthood, served as an eco-friendly governor; his then-youthful enthusiasm and interest in unconventional ways of thinking found him dubbed Governor Moonbeam and the name stuck (he was elected governor of the state again in 2010), contributing to California's forward-thinking identity. However, the Golden State's convergence of people and tolerance of outside philosophies, from the Hare Krishas, to Werner Erhard's est and Esalen, founded to further explore Aldous Huxley's concept of human potentiality, are also the source of much criticism and satire. Fraud, hokum, and pretentious are a few of the words that have been used to describe the quasi-religious scenes here (and similar accusations would await Jim Morrison). Among the key ingredients in this new mixture of native ritual, human potential movement, and merry-making, was the chemical compound, D-lysergic acid or LSD.

Acid Dreams

Aldous Huxley, known primarily as the author of *Brave New World*, used the futuristic world of 2025 to grapple with some of the issues of the early 20th Century. Extremely prophetic, much of Huxley's fictionalized society, consumed by pleasure-seeking and trivialities, seems to have been made real. In 1935, Huxley moved to California and began to study the ancient Hindu texts, the Vedas (from the Upshinads) leading to his interest in Vedanta; he fell in with Swami Prabhavanananda. Among his friends were novelists Christopher Ishwerwood and Ray Bradbury, as well as J. Krishnamurti of Madras, a philosophy and spiritual figure associated with the esoteric practice of Theosophy.

Southern California Hinduism

Following the arrival of Jiddu Krishnamurti to the Ojai Valley in the 1920s, and his series of spiritual awakenings which sent him around the world preaching his message – that revolution must take place in the mind – a wave of philosophies with roots in Hinduism hit America, and especially California, in the 1930s. Krishnamurti continued his practice and outreach for decades from his Southern California base; by the '80s, he was touting the ills of the world as a crisis in intellect. Decrying the emphasis placed on material values, he posited that more energy spent on educating youth could set societies back on track.

Following posts in San Francisco and Portland, Swami Prabhavananada arrived in Los Angeles where he founded the Vedanta Society of Southern California in 1930 (Aldous Huxley was a disciple; Christopher Isherwood and Prabhavanananda worked on a translation of the Bhagavad Gita). His teachings ultimately pointed toward the Eastern tradition of meditation as a tool, to enhance Christian prayer, improve Western life, and generally help East meet West.

Paramanhasa Yogananda established his Self-Realization Fellowship base in Los Angeles in 1925, where he lived until his death in 1952 (Yogananda is interred in Glendale). Self-Realization is a kind of marriage of Christianity and Hinduism, its goals to foster unity and goodwill among people across the world, with meditation among its core tools to enlightenment. Yogananda told his story in the widely read, *Autobiography of a Yogi*, first published in 1946. The Self-Realization Fellowship Lake Shrine, 17190 Sunset Blvd. in Pacific Palisades, though not specifically related to the Doors, is a pleasant stop along the Pacific Coast Highway between Santa Monica and Malibu. In addition to a manmade lake featuring turtles, fish, swan, and glorious vegetation, there sits religious monuments to all the major faiths, as well as a portion of Mahatma Gandhi's ashes. (A small private ceremony following the death of George Harrison was held onsite there). Self Realization also has a Hollywood Temple location on 4860 Sunset Blvd, adjacent to the Church of Scientology at 4810 Sunset Blvd.

In the late '50s, the Maharishi Mahesh Yogi arrived in California for the first time as part of his world tour, and at once began to collect celebrity followers. On subsequent visits in the early '60s, he opened his meditation centers and the practice caught on, thanks to a simplified approach he called Transcendental Meditation, based on his teacher Brahmananda Saraswatsi's

> method of Transcendental Deep Meditation. Maharishi founded the Students' International Meditation Society at UCLA in 1966 and gave talks on his practice at his center for the Spiritual Regeneration Movement Foundation; it is reportedly where Hollywood director David Lynch met him in the '70s. Lynch is the most visible disciple of Maharishi and carries on the work of proselytizing meditation practice through his David Lynch Foundation.

While exploring the outer limits of spirituality, Huxley made his living as a Hollywood screenwriter. By the '50s, he was experimenting with mescaline and LSD, chronicling his adventures in *The Doors of Perception*, though friends and fellow writers were largely not on board with his psychedelic forays. Initially falling into esoteric categories similar to yoga, hypnotism, mysticism, and psychology – practices limited to the fringe crowd– in the late 1950s, LSD was also the rage among the Hollywood elite. Actors were said to be administered it by their psychiatrists; most famously, the comedic leading man Cary Grant said the drug had brought him "inner peace." Additionally, the CIA was giving it to government personnel and unsuspecting people as part of their experiments in mind-control (codenamed, MK Ultra, the operation was later determined to be illegal). By 1963, the drug's positive properties were praised not only by Huxley who found, "…what came through the open door was the realization of love as the primary and fundamental cosmic fact," but by psychologist Timothy Leary and Al Hubbard, the drug's so-called Johnny Appleseed. There was also Owsley Stanley, also known as Bear, one of the primary LSD chemists and suppliers on the West Coast. Primarily known as a Bay Area figure, associated with the Grateful Dead and author Ken Kesey's Acid Tests, Owsley had passed through Los Angeles in 1965, leaving behind a trail of his substance before returning to San Francisco to take part in the massive psychedelic event. This has often served as explanation for how Jim Morrison and Ray Manzarek were on board for early Southern California trips, though more accurately: Any place in the US where there was a university science lab, there was generally acid to be found. Robby Krieger and John Densmore were also trippers, and while Morrison was not yet acquainted with the musicians, Ray knew John who knew Robby: they were in the same meditation class.

John Densmore grew up in West Los Angeles where he studied piano, but began to excel at music when he picked up the drumsticks. From University High School to the competitive Santa Monica City College marching band, Densmore drummed his way around the Westside. Liking the attention he received for it from girls was enough to sustain his interest in being a musician. A jazzman, he was tuned into Les McCann, John Coltrane, Miles Davis, and drummer, Elvin Jones. He occasionally found work at UCLA frat parties with his own jazz quartet, doing his best to swing like Jones. Frequenting clubs like Melody Lane on Adams Boulevard, "where no honkies ventured," as he puts it in his memoir, *Riders on the Storm*, he lived at home with his parents until his neighborhood was bulldozed to make way for the San Diego Freeway.

Central Avenue and the West Coast Blues

West Coast Blues, though not the most widely known strain of blues, was a relative latecomer to the blues game: A simplification of its history indicates it bloomed following the 1940s migration to California of Louisiana and Texas players who congregated at the clubs on LA's Central Avenue, home of the jazz and R&B scene. T-Bone Walker, Percy Mayfield, Amos Milburn, and Charles Brown were among the stellar names of West Coast Blues that also had a base in Northern California's Oakland (where Pee Wee Crayton and Lowell Fulson were the primary names). Bandleader Johnny Otis and his protégé Etta James did double duty in both Northern and Southern California's clubs and fostered associations and influence by living in both regions. Springing from Lionel Hampton's band to become an important West Coast bandleader in the rock 'n' roll era, Otis worked with Big Mama Thornton and Big Joe Turner, foundational R&B artists who during their later years made their homes in California.

The Doors didn't necessarily reflect the uptown style, swing, and urban electric blues (through a laidback California filter) the West Coast Blues sound brought, nor did they pluck their repertoire from California blues artists like Big Mama, though they, like she, performed the standard, "Rock Me" as performed by B.B. King. Like jazz, blues is about a foundational repertoire, and being able to jam, improvise, and innovate. As the Doors got to creating their own brand of psychedelic blues, they leaned into Chicago/Chess Records and the styles of Howlin' Wolf and Muddy Waters, and the boogie of John Lee Hooker, while absorbing the West Coast Blues in the air. One of the main venues offering blues to the counter-culture crowd was the Ash Grove on Melrose: From 1958-1973, the biggest names in blues and other traditional American music made appearances there, further interlacing traditional American music with the '60s LA rock crowd. Today, the blues survives in LA at small clubs like Cozy's, the Baked Potato, and the Mint, though it can occasionally be heard in higher profile rooms like House of Blues on Sunset Strip. A few nightspots in Inglewood and South LA still host blues legends and fans.

As for Central Avenue, formerly the center of African American culture in Los Angeles and home to its blues and jazz scene, it remains a hub of historic buildings and locations. The Dunbar Hotel, home to African American performers in the era of segregation, is both a Los Angeles and National Historic landmark; the Central Avenue Jazz Festival is an annual free music event. Fulfilling the legacy of the formerly thriving

> Central Avenue scene, today Leimart Park is at the center of African American cultural life in Los Angeles, with venues devoted to serving the local theater, poetry, blues, jazz, and in recent years, the hip hop communities.

By 1964, after the Beatles' invasion, like others of his generation, Densmore turned away from jazz and toward rock. He began to gravitate to the Sunset Strip where a series of venues catered to teenagers looking to see bands like the Byrds, Love, and the Rising Sons. He moved to Topanga Canyon, commuted to San Fernando Valley State College in Northridge, and tried LSD.

Points of the Diamond

With their minds, bodies, and spirits in some measure of alignment, in September of 1965, the Doors prepared to make their first recordings at World Pacific Recording Studios, headquarters of the Pacific Jazz label. Chet Baker, Gerry Mulligan, and Ravi Shankar were among the world-class artists on the Pacific label, founded by Dick Bock with whom Manzarek was acquainted through meditation. Bock had offered studio time to Rick and the Ravens and the Doors came to claim it. Morrison came up with the idea for the band name: He explained to the others that it came from Huxley's *The Doors of Perception*, that the author had taken his title from a line from *The Marriage of Heaven and Hell* by William Blake: This was not a Bibilcal Hell; rather it was an unbound, Dionysian state. "If the doors of perception were cleansed, everything would appear to man as it is—infinite."

For their first session, they laid down "Indian Summer" (the same song that surfaced later on *Morrison Hotel*). The second song attempted was "Moonlight Drive," (re-recorded for *Strange Days*). The remaining demo tracks were "Hello I Love You," "Summer's Almost Gone," "My Eyes Have Seen You," "End of the Night," and "Go Insane." Beginning the job of shopping the tape to record companies, all the major labels the band took meetings with passed on releasing them; one executive found "Go Insane" particularly distasteful, perceiving such a call for disorder as offense. ABC/Dunhill executive Lou Adler famously said there was "nothing he could use" on the demo tapes to which Morrison even more famously said, "It's ok, the Doors don't want to be used anyway." It was not a very auspicious start to a career on the Hollywood scene, and it was assurance of a non-invitation to the Adler-organized Monterey Pop Festival in 1967 where Jimi Hendrix, Otis Redding, Janis Joplin, and the Who all put in career-defining performances in June. In their stead the Adler-managed Mamas and the Papas performed; like the Doors they would go down in history as a group known for massive drama and drug problems with a singer who died (coincidentally, Jim and Mama Cass Elliot attended the same high school in Alexandria, Virginia).

Discouraged by the demo debacle and according to Densmore, Morrison's lack of professional experience, Ray's brothers Jim and Rick quit the band, and Robby Krieger got the call from Densmore to come down and sit in on guitar. He and Densmore were acquainted from their days at Uni High, following Krieger's return from Menlo School, a boys' prep in Northern California. Raised in Pacific Palisades, the guitarist grew up with music lessons and equipment, studied flamenco, dug the blues of Robert Johnson, and the folk music of Bob Dylan and the electric blues rock of Mike Bloomfield and Paul Butterfield. From coffeehouse gigs in jug bands like the Back Bay Chamberpot Terriers, to studying the sitar, Krieger took in a wide range of influence. Following a Chuck Berry gig at the Santa Monica Civic Auditorium, he surrendered his allegiance to Spanish classical guitar and bought his first electric, a Gibson SG. Densmore claims to have first turned on Kreiger on to acid; they formed the Psychedelic Rangers with a couple of friends following an LSD experience.

Following a series of lectures on the subject of consciousness-expanding meditation, in the spring of 1965, Krieger and Densmore were initiated into the world of devotees led by the Maharishi Mahesh Yogi who issued everyone a mantra, a unique word used for recitation during one's own private meditation practice. Beginning in 1959, Maharishi, as he was known to his followers, had traveled around the world, educating people on the healthful properties of meditation as a cure to "mind-chatter" and other ills associated with the material realm and the physical body. Los Angeles was among the cities Maharishi established one of his meditation centers in the early '60s. Between his arrival in the US and his association with the Beatles mid-decade, Maharishi wrote a book, *The Science of Being and the Art of Living* and toured the world spreading the word about yoga and his method of Transcendental Meditation, training teachers on location and his home base in Rishikesh, India. Ray Manzarek and Dorothy Fujikawa dropped in to one of Maharishi's outposts in Pacific Palisades and after a meditation session, Ray, who was seeking a drummer for Rick and the Ravens, introduced himself to Densmore and invited him to rehearse with the band at his parent's in Manhattan Beach. Ray was impressed with Robby's bottleneck blues style; his addition to "Moonlight Drive" was just the dreamy tag the song was lacking. For Ray, there were no accidents: Meditation was his three for three key to securing the points in what he called his "diamond."

Rehearsing in a space behind the Santa Monica Greyhound Bus Depot, the combination of Robby's folk and flamenco background, Ray's blues, jazz, and classical sense, and John's ability to improvise and feel the groove like a jazz player, meant the Doors could create songs as Jim worked out his lyrical jams. Everyone participated in the composition. "He came to our sessions with a piece of paper he'd scribbled some lyrics on," said Kreiger. "He was humming the music to it and we all started to work on the melodies," he says, explaining the band's collaborative process. So as to avoid sounding like the rest of the teenage/garage/British Invasion/blues-inspired rock bands of their era, the Doors chose to go bass-less, relying instead on Ray's left hand on the keyboards. There were problems with the approach: a number of the songs sounded similar with their bang of the organ, slide guitar, and jazz flicks of the drumsticks. To break the cycle, Jim gave everyone a directive; Go home and write a song based on one of the elements: earth, air, or water. Kreiger chose fire and brought it back to the band to finish, which is how Morrison came to add "and our love become a funeral pyre." Admittedly it was not his best lyric, but then "Light My Fire" was not Jim's song.

"He really wasn't musical," was Krieger's early impression of Morrison. But the tripper with the thousand-yard stare felt certain about one thing: "We never doubted for a minute that we were going to be big,"[3] he said. "We knew immediately that we had the best material of any group; we knew that we had the best-looking singer of any group. What could go wrong?"

Practicing on the beach, the Doors' next rehearsal space at 3811 Ocean Front Walk in Venice near Marina Del Ray was also where Ray and Dorothy lived. Paying to rehearse in the Manzareks' living space was not an arrangement that necessarily set well with the rest of the band, and one night Morrison notoriously trashed the place in a drunken haze. Despite petty power plays of that variety, the band played on, booking any gig they could get, from youth dances to private parties for Hollywood-types. By December they were signed to a limited contract with Columbia Records, agreeing to join up because they thought the label's rep, Billy James, was young, cool, and could hang around in style.

City of Night

The musician's life left days and late nights open for prowling around Venice and the greater Los Angeles area. Living among a population more tolerant and diverse than in Florida was a true revelation for Morrison: A place where matters of the mind and soul and people of many nations lived and loved more openly, where the physical beauty of the landscape met the tanned bodies of the bikini girls and muscle men, and where even the matronly were well-preserved. John Rechy's novel *City of Night* brought yet another side of LA life to light for Jim, and offered a taste of LA noir that Raymond Chandler had mostly left untouched. Published in 1963 by Grove Press, Rechy was not specifically a Beat, but his work is often associated with Allen Ginsberg, Gregory Corso, William Burroughs and Jack Kerouac. Specializing in covering aspects of the gay experience in a pre-tolerance era, Rechy's work was distinguished by his literary treatment of homosexual life, specifically his recollections of his own time as a street hustler. Rechy's outlaw visions encompassed the lives of wayward starlets and unsavory real life politicians alike. His was not a pulp fiction accounting; his gay-themed writings remain groundbreakers, taking in the full spectrum of human experience, from real love to self-hate. Rechy's non-judgmental understanding of the culture of narcissism and the way it thrives specifically in LA is among his unique contributions to literature.

Morrison shared these more obscure literary discoveries and his fresh insights with new buddy John Densmore – the singer providing the drummer with his library of influences and an introduction to poetry and philosophy. In turn, Densmore gave Morrison tutorials on the technical and improvisatory aspects of musical creativity, specifically the properties of jazz. Jim knew little to nothing about the music, but he dug the notion of free jazz from a poet's perspective. "Like Rimbaud and 'the derangement of the senses,'"[4] he noted while Densmore explained the rudiments of clutching the root and feeling the music, the tool of the free-stylist. These seeds of influence – from

German philosophy, mescaline experimentation, and the chaotic sensations inspired by blues and jazz themes – were not ideas flooding the average teenage head on his way to Sunset Strip, but they were surely percolating in the mind of Morrison who was waiting for a chance to pop, dying to make a connection with humanity and leave his marks on the arts.

"That's why poetry appeals to me so much – because it's so eternal," he would say, in later years. "As long as there are people, they can remember words and combinations of words: nothing else can survive a holocaust but poetry and songs. But so long as there are human beings, songs and poetry can continue."[5]

Alongside their artistic discovery, Densmore and Morrison were also girl crazy guys, haunting the clubs and nightspots, from Venice West Café at 7 Dudley Avenue, to Olivia's restaurant on the corner of Main Street and Ocean Park (today it's ZJ Boarding House, a surf and skate supply store serving Dogtown, the epicenter of California skateboarding activity). Olivia's was a soul food restaurant and a hangout for locals and artists, UCLA film students, and musicians, including Linda Ronstadt and the Stone Poneys. Its warm vibe, student-right prices, and atypical Southern-styled meals on the Westside, made the place the inspiration for the song "Soul Kitchen," though its real origins are buried in Jim's past and yet another memory of Mary Werbelow.

Your fingers weave quick minarets
Speak in secret alphabets
I light another cigarette
Learn to forget

Jim would need to "learn to forget" his time with Mary in Clearwater and their game of matchsticks, ending on a bet that Jim lost the day they met. He would need to forget that day he washed her car, had his haircut at her request, and dropped her off at the movies, which he remembered was *West Side Story*. Forget the next three years after that, life as a couple, soul mates, Jim reciting poetry to her, especially William Blake. Learn to forget that she was his first audience, the first person with whom he could truly share himself, as well as his enthusiasm for the writing of Burroughs, Kerouac, Mailer, Rimbaud, Huxley, Nitzsche, Marx, and the paintings of Hieronymous Bosch. Learn to forget that he'd ask her to speak to him only in rhyme, or that whenever he took the driver's seat, he'd hand her his notebook, asking her to take down whatever he dictated, so as to keep his hands upon the wheel. Forget that she'd moved to Los Angeles, just to be with him, and that he ultimately betrayed her, even though he claimed to love Mary, and probably still did.[6]

But she was gone. Jim was just one of the guys now, a singer, a songwriter, a member of the Doors. He hadn't been so alone in some time. In his limbo state, he made the mistake of writing to his family, now stationed in London, to tell them he was thinking of joining a band. Admiral Morrison replied, stating the idea was preposterous. Years later his father would say, "We never knew he sung."

CHAPTER 3

Sunset Strip: 1966-1967

It was Jim's idea to take a trip to Mexico with friends in early 1966, but they only got as far as Needles before the drunk and disorderly conduct set in: Originally on the search for peyote, Morrison became deranged and disoriented on the road to the point of no return. Retreating to LA, his senses in a disturbed and rearranged state, and at risk of arrest for jeopardizing the lives of his traveling companions, the wild ride to the desert illustrates just another day in the life of Jim Morrison: By early 1966 the ceremony had officially begun.

The Doors launched their first month-long residency at The London Fog, a "dingy, nautical-themed" club at 8919 Sunset Boulevard that didn't get quite as much action as some of the other spots on the world-famous Sunset Strip. Billed as "The Doors from Venice," the members of the band were the new kids on the blocks that housed The Sea Witch (8516 Sunset), Ciro's (8433 Sunset), the Whisky A-Go Go (8901 Sunset), and a number of other old school drinking establishments the new generation was turning into its own.

Initial fame to the area came by way of the hit TV show, *77 Sunset Strip*, followed by the establishment of the Whisky, as it was known then. As one of the first discotheques in the United States, it had a female DJ, perched in a cage, which devolved into girls dancing behind bars, birthing the go-go dancing craze. By 1966, the go-go girls were gone, replaced by hippies who made the scene for the Whisky's rock acts: The Byrds, Buffalo Springfield, and Love. Arthur Lee of Love would go on to write a song about the scene: "Maybe the People Would Be the Times or Between Park and Hilldale." *And here, they always play my songs*, he sang.

"Arthur Lee and Love: They were in charge," said Ray Manzarek. "We wanted to be like Love."[1] He and Morrison would watch Love's set from the wings at the Whisky on their break; Arthur Lee would do the same, taking in the Doors at the London Fog. "Sometimes, during our breaks, I would go down and check them out," wrote Lee in his memoir. "…I found Jim to be very interesting… after awhile, with Ray playing the organ, I could see that they were doing something quite different."[2]

Arthur Lee was originally from Memphis but was raised in the West Adams district of Los Angeles; legend had it he would walk to Hollywood from his home as a kid, taking in the scenery, soaking up the vibes of central LA. By the mid-'60s Lee was pretty much a free-spirit/Californian all the way. He and his friend Johnny Echols formed their first bands in high school and played in various formations while Lee worked on his songwriting diligently: his "My Diary" for Rosa Lee Brooks is famous as an early session of guitarist Jimi Hendrix who Lee had seen in a show-stopping performance with the Isley Brothers. By 1965, right around the time the Byrds were achieving notoriety for their jingle-jangle folk-rock sound, Lee was ready to unleash the complex symphony of sound that had been clanging around in his head and enter the folk-rock race.

Like Manzarek, Morrison had set his sights on being at least as big as Love. But Lee had a major lead on Morrison and the Doors on the Sunset Strip scene: Love had signed to Elektra Records and the record was to be released imminently. Living in a castle in Laurel Canyon, Lee was already dating the area's ladies, Pamela Courson among them. Morrison was determined to cut a figure like Arthur Lee, someone who maintained an air of mystery behind his well-developed musical ideas; a powerful performer, he delivered a mixture of cool and flair. There was another element to Lee's profile that set him apart from the crowd on the Strip: calling himself "the first black hippie," Lee reveled in his outsider status among blacks and whites. Like Seattle's Jimi Hendrix and Northern California's Sly Stone, Lee's way-out western failure to fit in was the strength of his songs and at the core of his character – a character that Morrison recognized in his own search for an identity as a performer, and maybe even as a man.

"I thought Jim was a lonely person. He was searching. Now that I think about it and put it all together, it seemed like he didn't have a self," said Arthur Lee, written many years down the road.

At the time Lee encountered them on the Strip, the Doors were still just the little band from Venice. Unlike Love who played to packed houses of exuberant teenagers at the more desirable Whisky, the Doors' London Fog shows were performed for an audience of passerby, a group of rag tag drunks, and a go-go dancer no longer in her prime.

Everyone who saw them at the time recalls Morrison's posture as "slumped," "standing in the corner," "with his back to the audience." Still shy and reticent, unless plied with substances, he hadn't yet developed any kind of stage technique or a persona, despite his interest in theatrics. In an effort to make the onstage hours more interesting, the band developed some meandering passages that would eventually become their trademark jams: Ironically, the deadbeat gig at the London Fog produced the defining instrumental stretches of "Light My Fire" and "The End." The idea to stretch out came from seeing Love, "The first band I ever saw playing long improvisational songs,"[3] said Manzarek.

From Thursday to Sunday from nine in the evening until two in the morning, and eventually on Tuesdays and Wednesdays, earning each member $15 a night, the Doors developed an act. It was during their London Fog stand that Morrison spied the aforementioned Pamela Courson, talking to John Densmore. A high school dropout, enrolled in art classes at Los Angeles City college, in short order Pam became Jim's paramour and would remain so on and off for the next five years. Those who knew her during her young life on the LA scene have stated for the record she hadn't developed much of a life direction or personality; many of them recall her red head of hair, that she had a bit of a mean streak, and an even meaner drug addiction, which eventually killed her in 1974. Much has been written on Morrison and Courson's star-crossed relationship; for the purpose of this telling, whatever influence she may've had on Morrison and his creativity will go unexplored.

The Whisky and the Sunset Strip

The first club named Whisky A Go Go was opened in Paris in 1953, under the auspice of Regine Zybelberg, the empress of Parisian nightlife. Credited with the idea of replacing the typical nightclub jukebox with two turntables, Regine's invention facilitated *musique non-stop*. In 1958, the Whisky A Go Go in Chicago, no relation to Regine's as her places became known, became designated as the first discotheque in America. By 1964 entrepreneurs Elmer Valentine, Phil Tanzini, Shelly Davis, and Theodore Flier used the Whisky A Go Go name, again, no relation to the Whisky in Chicago or Regine's, and took things to the next level with their club on the Sunset Strip with its live DJ, go-go girls, and Johnny Rivers as a fixture. In 1966, an offshoot of the Chicago club opened in D.C., sparking Whisky franchise locations in other locales and a kind of nationwide go-go dancing consciousness, helped along by nationally syndicated shows like *Hullabaloo*. Following the club's '60s stand as the premier showcase for California rock and touring bands, in later years the Strip and the Whisky scene was revived by glam and punk rockers, heavy metal hair bands, and pay-to-play local acts. The Whisky remains the nightclub of longest standing on the Strip from the original '60s era, still operating alongside more contemporary nightspots like the Dan Akroyd-owned House of Blues, the Johnny Depp-founded

> Viper Room, and the Comedy Store that launched David Letterman, Jay Leno, and Roseanne Barr, among other comedians. The famous photo of the Doors atop a billboard advertising their album was also located at 8171 Sunset Boulevard.

By May, the awkward "The Doors from Venice" had become more polished as the Doors. Invited by the Whisky's booking agent Ronnie Haran to become the house band, they opened shows there, five nights a week. Earning $500, about twice what they were paid weekly by the London Fog, in 1966, the Doors played in front of just about every band that crossed the club's threshold: "The Rascals, Paul Butterfield, the Turtles, the Seeds, Frank Zappa and the Mothers of Invention, Them, the Animals, the Beau Brummels, Buffalo Springfield, and Captain Beefheart." With the increased stage time and audience exposure came more critical reviews. Panned by the *LA Times* which described them as "disheveled" and "lost in their own world," the group took it as sign that if the establishment hated them, they must be doing something right. In less than a year, the Doors had become official ambassadors of a new underground ethos. With a pervading aura of chaos, Morrison's aim toward disrupting, disturbing, and awakening people, while discouraging conforming to societal mores, was an artistic directive very much in synch sync with his times. Poet Ed Sanders (member of counterculture musical collective the Fugs) called Morrison, on one hand, "an American Rock and Roll Bacchus, and on the other a canny performer, who used his musical/literary abilities to please and rouse up a Rebellious Generation."[4] The Doors were no squeaky-clean representatives of beachy California; rather, they were its inversion. Their serious expressions, roughish appearance, and minor chords were a world away from the fun, fun, fun of the Beach Boys or Jan and Dean's "Little Old Lady From Pasadena." Certainly, they were the only band from the Pacific shore to quote from Céline, using the savage, nihilistic imagery of his *Voyage au bout de la nuit* as a jumping off point for a song, as in their "End of the Night."

Perceived as just too far-out by the corporate suits at Columbia who elected to drop them from their development deal, and ignored by other labels who didn't know what to do with an act so outside the mainstream, there exist various accounts of how the Doors came to the attention of the far more progressive concern, Elektra Records and its chief, Jac Holzman. In one version, Holzman's wife Nina sees the Doors at the London Fog; in another, Ronnie Haran of the Whisky, responsible for turning on Holzman to Love, gets him to the club again to see the Doors. Another story says that it was Arthur Lee who told Holzman that while visiting California, he'd better catch the Doors.

Holzman had founded his record label with $300 and a friend, while a student at St. John's College in 1950; its very name, Elektra, is derived from one of the Seven Sisters of Greek mythology. The label's first release was a collection of Lieder – German poems set to music – followed by a who's who of folk artists with largely leftist, political repertoire, a style of music for which Elektra would became known. But Holzman had recently and successfully made the switch from folk-centered artists like Judy Collins, Phil Ochs, and Tom Paxton by signing Love and the Paul Butterfield Blues Band from the LA scene. When he got to the Doors' show, at first he didn't know what to make of them; he didn't get them at all. Given the common ground, there was not a chance he was tone deaf to the Doors' points of reference and views – they simply weren't delivering. "Arthur had a high opinion of them and I had a very high opinion of Arthur's opinion so I stayed," Holzman wrote in his memoir *Follow the Music*. Returning a few nights running, "Finally, the fourth evening, I heard them," he wrote. "Jim generated an enormous tension with his energy, like a black hole, sucking the energy of the room into himself." He recognized Densmore's improvisational skills and ability to follow Jim. He heard Manzarek's discipline, and the baroque stylings; he appreciated Kreiger's unique tone, and hoped a minimalist approach with Jim's voice in the mix would blend in much the same way the artists he'd produced in the folk vein had. And then he set about collecting opinions and feedback from insiders whose tastes he respected.[5] Among them was Elektra house producer, Paul Rothchild, who though initially not a fan, was eventually won over by the Doors in performance. "At the same time they were awful, I could tell they were very different from anything I'd heard before," Rothchild told *BAM* magazine. "I had nothing to relate them to. They were totally unique."[6]

The Doors signing with Elektra in August of 1966, coincided with their final performance at the Whisky after a good, solid run. High on an inconceivable amount of LSD, the rest of the band had to chase down their lead singer and wake him out of a stupor at his nearby hideout, the Alta Cienega Motel. Flying on an acid trip that had gone beyond all reasonable bounds, the band pulled Jim together and walked him over to the club; they got to the door and walked him onstage. By the time they reached the end of the set and traditional jam on "The End," the band didn't know it yet, but Morrison was going to spontaneously perform a new section of the song as it climaxed.

Father....I want to kill you
Mother....I want to....

It was all the owners of the Whisky needed to hear: fired on the spot, the Doors were asked to complete their weekend shows, and to never return.

Sunset Sound

Sessions for the Doors' debut album occurred over six days in August 1966 at Sunset Sound Recorders, 6650 Sunset Boulevard, with producer Paul Rothchild and engineer Bruce Botnick. It had been just over a year since Jim and Ray met on the beach and had begun to write songs; with John and Robby in the group, they were able to pull together a real repertoire. There were flashes of their beloved jazz and baroque on "Light My Fire;" the blues were represented by Willie Dixon's "Back Door Man" and "Break on Through" which took its cues from "Mellow Down Easy," as recorded by the Paul Butterfield Blues Band. There were completely original tunes like "Crystal Ship" (a goodbye song to Mary that fit no mold), alongside theatrical pieces like "Alabama Song" (Dorothy

Fujikawa suggested the band record it; the "whisky bar" lyric was just a happy accident). "Take It As It Comes," came from a phrase borrowed from the spiritual teachings of the Maharishi Mahesh Yogi: the Doors' song uses the phrase to extol the thrill of prolonged lovemaking. Though The Beatles were most often associated with the pint-sized guru with the unmistakably squeaky voice and high-pitched giggle, the Doors were actually among his earliest devotees in rock.

It was decided in the studio that "The End" was to be among the focal points of the album. What had begun as an extended live jam was about to be enshrined as one of the band's most enduring recorded tracks. "It was very popular to do long songs at the time," said Doors' engineer Bruce Botnick. "It was the thing to do."[7] Working on the Doors' debut and Love's second album, *Da Capo*, simultaneously, Botnick and producer Paul Rothchild (newly released from jail after having taken a rap on drug charges) oversaw the creation of Love's "Revelation." The 20-minute excursion took up the entirety of side two of *Da Capo*, issued at the beginning of 1967 alongside *The Doors*. "It was one of the most beautiful moments I've ever had in a recording studio," said Rothchild. "That half hour when 'The End' was recorded."[8]

As the story goes, "The End" was cut over two nights, and at the end of the second session, Morrison snuck into the recording studio and hosed it with a fire extinguisher, believing it necessary to "cool the place down." For Morrison, nothing could top that studio session: After recording "The End" and the later epic, "When the Music's Over," he said the performances became static. The songs had evolved from improvisational numbers in the set, "freeform pieces," he explained. "But once we put them on record, they just kind of stopped. They were kind of at the height of their effect anyway so it didn't really matter."[9]

At first Morrison characterized "The End" as a goodbye song, then added, "I think it's sufficiently complex and universal in its imagery that it could be almost anything you want it to be." He once told a friend "The End" was about the demise of their friendship and their aborted trip to Mexico. But what began as a send-off, inspired by what was perceived to be his abandonment by Mary Werbelow out West, ultimately peered into worlds lesser known: "The End" was truly the revelation and beginning of not only an outrageous career, but of Morrison's deeper explorations into the realm Carl Jung called collective unconscious. With its connection to the timeless, and specifically the myth of Oedipus Rex, "The End" is steeped in subconscious material and is a story as old and universal as time. Supporting human experience for millennia, according to scholar Joseph Campbell, the myths offer clues "to our spiritual nature and could help guide us to a sacred place within where we might unlock the creative power of our deeper unconscious self," or what he calls "the rapture of being alive."[10] "You either say yes to the serpent or no to the serpent," said Jung. The serpent, "a perfect emblem of the Selfhood…imprisoned in its own cycle of death and rebirth"[11] is also at once a symbol of medicine and poison, and a sign of life.

By the end of 1966, the Doors were fully animated: Jim moved to Laurel Canyon with Pamela Courson, though he never gave up his favorite spots like the Alta Cienega where he bunked down on nights he didn't feel like going home. Before the year was through, the band had taken its first trip to New York to sit in on the mixing of their album with Paul Rothchild, and to play a residency at the nightclub, Ondine, where New York's hippest – the art crowd – turned out and largely embraced LA's new thing. The Doors were feeling good about what had been achieved. "We were hot," said Kreiger. "It was then that we realized we were different from other groups," said Morrison. "We were making music that would last for years, not weeks."

CHAPTER 4
Strange Days Have Found Him: 1967

Though "Break on Through" was a powerful and energetic single, and even had an early version of a music video – a promotional film – to accompany it, *The Doors* was released without much fanfare in January of 1967. "Break on Through" didn't catch fire with the listening audience and didn't get much radio airplay; it didn't even crack the Billboard Hot 100, the measure of a single's success at the time. But the Doors were loved by the newly established rock press, especially by *Crawdaddy!*, the first American underground rock 'n' roll magazine, which reviewed the album in issue #9. "*The Doors* is an album of magnitude," wrote the magazine's founder and editor, Paul Williams. "Thanks to the calm surefootedness of the group, the producer, the record company, there are no flaws: The Doors have been delivered to the public full grown (by current standards) and still growing (standards change). Gestation may've been long and painful. No one cares. The birth of the group is in this album and it's as good as anything in rock."[1]

As *The Doors* made its splash in the press and the members of the band continued to make the scene, Morrison was pursuing his own routine: drinking excessively, dropping acid imperviously, living at night, inside and out, from the Westside's beaches to Westwood's movie houses. There is a story that circulates from this period: Upon exiting a theater after one of his usual screenings, a young woman recognized Jim on the street and exchanged words with him. "The End," had profoundly affected her, she told him. So much so, she was now a psychiatric patient, on a walk with her nurse from a nearby hospital.

"I didn't realize people took songs so seriously and it made me wonder whether I ought to consider the consequences," said Morrison, recalling the incident for an interviewer. "…You don't think of the consequences and you can't."[2]

In this early part of 1967, the Doors as a band were still very much developing their stage act. Putting in appearances on the East Coast and West Coast, up and down the state and across Hollywood, from the Hullabaloo to the newly opened Gazzarri's (where Mary Werbelow found work as a dancer)[3], the band drew its biggest crowd on home turf to date at South Santa Monica's Cheetah Club, on the pier at Pacific Ocean Park.

Pacific Ocean Park and Santa Monica Civic Auditorium

Members of the '60s generation will primarily remember the Cheetah Club as being on the same pier as Pacific Ocean Park, which operated from 1958 to 1967, and was generally located between the two large white apartment blocks between Ocean Park and Marine on the Venice border. An area intensive with historic piers and amusements, from the early 20th Century until the '70s, pier after pier – the Crystal Pier, the Pickering Pier and Frazier's Million Dollar pier – was built in the Ocean Park area of Santa Monica, then burned to the ground. The Lick Pier, which dates back to 1925, was home to the Aragon Ballroom, primarily known as the place where bandleader Lawrence Welk and his dancers broadcast its show during the '50s; in 1967, it became the Cheetah Club, attracting regional bands like the Doors, the Mothers of Invention, the Seeds, and Love, as well as touring bands like Pink Floyd. The dilapidated club contributed to the abandoned pier's seedy seaside vibe; it stopped operating in about 1968-69 and finally burned to the ground in 1970.

Santa Monica Civic Auditorium at 1855 Main Street in Santa Monica is a piece of distinctly Southern California architecture and is the area's remaining historic rock 'n' roll venue. Designed by Welton Beckett – the architect famous for the Capitol Records stack of records building, the Beverly Hilton Hotel, and the Los Angeles Music Center, among other highly visible structures around LA and the world – Santa Monica Civic opened in 1958. The 3,000-seat venue is known to rock fans for

> hosting historic appearances by the Beach Boys, Bob Dylan, Led Zeppelin, Bruce Springsteen, and the Clash, among many others. Today, the stage receives fewer rock 'n' roll workouts and is used mostly for trade shows and city events.[4]

The Doors were also building an audience at the Fillmore, the Avalon, and other psychedelic ballrooms of San Francisco. Among the band's earliest surviving live concert tapes are the performances in March of 1967 from their stand at the Matrix (the club owned by the Jefferson Airplane's Marty Balin). Following *The Doors* release, but before "Light My Fire" had penetrated the charts, the tapes reveal a band very much in control, performing to a small but contained crowd. But the live version of "Light My Fire" recorded at the Matrix also demonstrates the band's ability to cut loose and improvise. They could swing with a beat that bent the roots of rock 'n' roll, and could get nearly New Orleanian with their good time roll (slipping into "Get Outta My Life Woman," an actual New Orleans groove, written by Allen Toussaint and made famous by Lee Dorsey). They reached back in time with a cover of "Money," the 1958 hit by Barrett Strong for the Tamla Records imprint of Motown. The Beatles' frenzied version, bursting with sound, was considered to be among the first "heavy rock" songs; in the hands of the Doors, it was performed weirdly slowed down, taking its cues from John Lee Hooker's blues and replacing their own wild and abandoned sound with the swirl of his one-note boogie-drone. Among the songs the Doors performed at the time, about a third are credited to blues and first wave of rock 'n' roll writers. The rest of the set is devoted to originals and theatrical interpretations – Gershwin's "Summertime" and Brecht/Weill's "Alabama Song" – and one contemporary cover of "Gloria" by Them, the Irish group also steeped in the blues. Them's lead singer Van Morrison enjoyed a brotherly camaraderie with the other Morrison during their brief acquaintance: They caroused, joking that perhaps they were cousins or brothers from another mother. Their fast friendship stoked the fires of legend when both Morrisons frequently spoke fondly of the night their bands jammed at the Whisky on "Gloria" and Wilson Pickett's "In the Midnight Hour," in the summer of 1966.

On another occasion, a gig with the Grateful Dead insured that some of Owsley's most potent purple acid found its way into Morrison's hands (the underground chemist loved to personally gift the new lords of rock with his goods). For the first part of 1967, Jim was soaking in substances, and that's exactly how he entered Sunset Sound to record the Doors' second album, to be titled *Strange Days*. But by April, the song Jim originally issued as an assignment to his bandmates, to write about one of the elements, had gone and set the night on fire. The ubiquitous "Light My Fire" blared from every jukebox, bedroom turntable, car, and transistor radio. Word got out that the band was officially hot. Jimi Hendrix, on his way out West, stopped by Steve Paul's Scene in New York to check in with the band. On continuous dates, from coast to coast and up and down California, the sudden surge in interest preempted the studio time booked and necessitated securing professional (though short-lived) management. But there was no longer any doubt who was on the rise or who were the new crowned kings of the LA scene. Their once overlooked debut had become their commercial breakthrough and big artistic statement, a blueprint for the Doors' dark and brooding, "original blues."

Performing throughout the 1967 concert season at a strange mix of high school auditoriums and fairgrounds, the Doors became part of the psychedelic soundtrack to the celebrated Summer of Love. So aligned were they with the hippie migration and its sound, the Doors were sometimes mistaken for being a part of the acid rock movement coming out of San Francisco. During their appearance on *American Bandstand,* and following their performance of "Crystal Ship," host Dick Clark took the opportunity to clarify the band's origins and ask, "Why is so much happening in San Francisco? You figured it out yet?" Morrison didn't miss a beat. "The West is the Best," he said, quoting himself and "The End," before famously closing with "Light My Fire," potentially incendiary for containing the word "higher," which remained unapproved-by-network-standards.

In contrast to the flower power sounds surrounding them, the Doors and their more somber moods gave one reviewer cause to declare them "carnivores in a land of musical vegetarians." Such a dissonance between artists with underground influences and inclinations, and the mentality of the mainstream, was not uncommon; despite their hit status, the Doors were often misunderstood. There was also the matter of an East versus West Coast sensibility: Boston folk, Eastern seaboard prep, and gritty urban art rock a la the Velvet Underground, versus the wild and loose psychedelia favored by the sun-soaked and water-logged Western set.

In August of 1967, the Doors showed up for one of their all time oddest bookings: Opening for Simon and Garfunkel in Forest Hills, New York, on the site of the US Open tennis tournament. Though "Light My Fire" had officially reached the number one spot on the hit parade on July 25, the kids turned out in droves for the folky duo, of "Sounds of Silence" fame, clad in their cable knit sweaters. The pair hadn't yet released "Mrs. Robinson" and their breezy soundtrack to *The Graduate*, but the duo's success compared to the Doors' icy reception at the Forest Hills gig was a clear case of home court advantage. Another weird line-up at the height of "Light My Fire" fame occurred at Jim's old high school in Alexandria, Virginia, on a bill shared with The Tokens, most famous for "The Lion Sleeps Tonight," their doo-wop version of the South African tune originally popularized as "Wimoweh" by the Weavers. Such strange juxtapositions characterized rock 'n' roll in the '60s, especially in regions that had not yet caught up to the new sounds from the West Coast. Early years in the mind expansion game, among the young generation there was still a subset of youth unready and unaccepting of the language and performance of Jim and his Morrison-isms, the energies he and the Doors unleashing still strange and frightening to them. They would eventually catch-up.

When recording of *Strange Days* finally resumed at Sunset Sound, the album's kaleidoscopic, sonic circus became a reflection of the on-the-road weirdness the band faced and embraced.

Cancel my subscription to the resurrection
Send my credentials to the house of detention
I got some friends inside

It was in this period when Jim grew increasingly unreliable; he developed habits like "skipping out of the studio on breaks and getting hammered," according to one succinct account on the Doors' online timeline. But besides the interruptions and escalating bouts of drunkenness, creativity was at a peak. In just two takes, the band cut "When the Music's Over," one of their most enduring tracks. The sessions also sparked another classic in "Love Me Two Times." Krieger got the strange ping from his guitar by hammering the third string, a trick he also used on "Back Door Man." His touch was an emulation of Muddy Waters' electric slide style.

By high summer, the Doors were headlining the Santa Monica Civic Auditorium performing to an audience of 3000 and breaking their own attendance records.[5] Expanding their tour itinerary, they lit out for dates in the Midwest.

In August 1967, the shocking news came through that Beatles manager Brian Epstein had passed away overnight while his band was in India at the Maharishi's mediation retreat. The Doors heard the news directly from Derek Taylor, the press agent they shared with the Beatles. As the entire music world mourned Epstein's passing, Maharishi and Transcendental Meditation became headline news. Suddenly, the power source of the Doors' initial connection, the hook-up in their mystical formation, as well as TM, the tool they used for maintaining focus, was no longer "their little secret."

As the summer raged on, Jim and the Velvet Underground's singer Nico fell for each other. Following an introduction at Love's Hollywood residence the Castle, the pair ran off together for a brief affair to share peyote buttons and write under the desert sky. Jim collaborated with Nico on verses she eventually turned into songs, like the dark and spacey "Lawns of Dawns," but their liaison would not be for long: Wandering spirits, respective addictions, and distinctly separate careers deterred the artists from having anything that could be termed a relationship.

The Doors released their second album of the year in September: *Strange Days* was comprised mostly of songs leftover from the '65-'66 writing sessions, including "Moonlight Drive," the very first song Jim tried out on Ray at the beach. "Horse Latitudes" was another one with some miles on it; one of Jim's earliest poems, it came straight from the notebook he carried with him from Florida to California.

When the still sea conspires an armor
And her sullen and aborted currents breed tiny monsters
True sailing is dead

The album title is perfectly suited to the overall psychedelic mood: The title song was evocative of Morrison's experiences in New York. Among the first rock musicians to play the Moog synthesizer, Manzarek's eerie and classic modes, as well as his harpsichord throughout, matched the surreal images of circus performers on the cover. The photos by Joel Brodsky were taken on New York streets, the entire package a piece in tune with the times, in the immediate fall following the Summer of Love.

"People Are Strange" made its unpolished debut in September of 1967 on *The Ed Sullivan Show* where the Doors were also slated to perform their massive hit, "Light My Fire." The show had a history of asking rock 'n' roll artists like Bo Diddley, Buddy Holly, Bob Dylan, and the Rolling Stones to adjust their repertoire to suit the host and his censors; Dylan went as far as to walk off the set. Jim handled it differently: Though as usual he'd been asked to change the lyric, he went ahead and sang "girl we couldn't get much higher." The move effectively ended the band's relationship with the *Sullivan* show.

Further strange days awaited Morrison and Co. on the East Coast when they made an inexplicably bizarre clip for "People Are Strange." Performing in a vignette meant for broadcast on DJ Murray the K's network TV show, the scenario includes lip-synching, extras outfitted in wigs and nylon stockings on their heads, a team of women enacting a stick-up of the US Treasury, and the theft of a medallion straight from Morrison's neck, plucked by a sexy space alien on the passenger side of the getaway car.

The New York trip also included a rather notoriously awkward meeting with Andy Warhol. The pop artist presented Jim with the most peculiar gift of a garish, baroque telephone. It was a kind gesture, but Morrison's style and preference in people and party favors were much more root-bound: He spurned the Warhol crowd for a chance to hang out with blues-rock band Canned Heat, friends from LA who were on their own New York run.

When *Strange Days* hit the shelves in October, *The Doors* was still resting on a perch in the Top 10. Reaching only the top three position on the charts, *Strange Days* was considered a disappointment (for not matching or exceeding the debut album's sales success). And yet, from a critical and artistic perspective, it is among the Door's finest. "It ventures beyond the conventional realm of musical expression: it has become the theater," noted *The Los Angeles Free Press* at the time. "Strange Days," "When You're Strange," and "Moonlight Drive" remain exemplary Summer of Love works in a canon-full of psychedelic mastery.

That same month in 1967, *Rolling Stone* made its debut at newsstands; becoming rock 'n' roll culture's periodical of record, the magazine would go on to cover the Doors extensively. The band was simultaneously a favorite at *16 Magazine*, geared as it was toward younger readers, specifically girls and the pop charts. The photo shoot organized by the teenybopper magazine's editor, Gloria Stavers, is often credited for turning Morrison (among other musicians) into a sex symbol. A photo spread of Jim also appeared in *Vogue*, further enhancing his appeal as the band played on, riding high on the successes of the first album and the more expansive *Strange Days*.

By the end of the year, reeling from the demands and the pace of the spotlight, Morrison took exception to the tight security at a concert arena in New Haven. Voicing his objections in an alleged "obscene" manner, he confronted police backstage, as well as onstage. The police returned his verbal ire with force: while kissing a girl in his own dressing room, he was sprayed in the face with mace. Onstage, Morrison retold the backstage events in a verse: "Little blue man, in the little blue hat…the little blue pig." He was sprayed by mace again as he resisted arrest onstage and the FBI opened a file on him.

Rolling Stone reported the incident in New Haven in its January 20, 1968 issue: "Mace is the same anti-personnel spray used by Oakland police during the October anti-draft demonstrations." The brutal attempt to thwart youth expression and to subdue Jim Morrison and other charismatic rock figures was in full effect, less than six months since the so-called Summer of Love. There would be more, even stranger days on the Doors' horizon, and Jim would of course be at center stage.

CHAPTER 5

Shaman's Blues: 1968

By his own admission, John Densmore hated the blues and remained unaware, at the time, what Jim was gleaning from his immersion in the music. "He was obsessed with the way black blues singers sounded. The raw feeling of pain expressed in their voices seemed to reverberate in him. He listened intently, lost in his own world," Densmore came to understand.

Wresting far more from the music than its surface-level moans and aches, Morrison recognized in the blues the range of emotions, written in carefully rendered rhyme schemes and secret alphabets. Its picaresque stories of midnight creeps, naïve boss men, and other men's women, had mystical elements and curative properties – the very things he went seeking in occult books and a bottle of beer or ten, the bluesmen had sought too. The music was a balm for an aching spirit and a cry for love, as it coursed through the night, celebrating life. From the heart of the city, down the mountain and though the canyon, from the beach and the Bay to dry desert land, Morrison felt the blues in LA's stories, and tried to bring that sensibility to the band.

It was only natural that Morrison should study the blues: All the great rock singers had learned from it. Without the blues, there was no Bo Diddley, no Elvis, no Beatles, no Tina Turner, no Rolling Stones. Bob Dylan emerged, and then went electric with his version of it; Jimi Hendrix was a veteran of its club circuit, and psychedelic Texan, Janis Joplin, had taken inspiration from its women: Bessie Smith, Billie Holiday, Etta James, and Big Mama Thornton. The Who were sprung from Maximum R&B, the Animals had Northern soul, and the British guitarists, Eric Clapton, Jimmy Page, and Jeff Beck, relied on blues roots for their source. Without the blues, there was no Love for the Doors to aspire to be like, nor any other LA garage band to fill the clubs on Sunset Strip. The blues was everything. Though contrary to popular belief, the blues is not a reflection of a state of depression; rather, its songs are a celebration of life, a pursuit of things unseen and beyond it, an assertion that one can find satisfaction in the soul, a place to call home in a world that may be beyond redemption. It is a consolation, like religion or philosophy. Like his literary heroes – most famously Arthur Rimbaud and William Blake, as well as his beloved Beats – Morrison went in search of the meaningful with a veracity that would not rest, and the blues was an essential part of that exploration.

"I like singing blues," Morrison explained in later years. "These free long blues trips, where there's no specific beginning or end. It just gets into a groove and I can just keep making up things. And everybody's soloing. I like that kind of song rather than just a *song*,"[1] he said. It was something he was hoping to experiment with on the band's third album: he planned to wrestle down his poem, "Celebration of the Lizard," and turn it into a song.

Manzarek's blues perspectives were similarly unformed: One need only listen to the organ lines of "Back Door Man," "Soul Kitchen", and "When the Music's Over" in sequence to hear evidence of his limitations. Ironically, Manzarek's primary framework for composition was more complex – European classical and American classical (jazz), though Chicago blues was in his toolkit, by virtue of his upbringing there.

"I always liked jazz but once I heard the blues I was hooked," Manzarek told *Rolling Stone* some time after the Doors were through. "What I learned from were those Southside Chicago blues. You've got to know when to play, how much to play, and when you get out. You've got to be succinct in your ideas."[2]

One of the clearest ideas the Doors brought to their blues-based music was Mazarek's left hand on the Fender Rhodes: It was the band's secret weapon, and it differentiated the group from the rest of the Sunset Strip garage bands. Going bass-less was what had set them apart from the other bands of white boys who sang the blues (though a charismatic singer the likes of Jim didn't hurt). With contemporaries like Paul Butterfield Blues Band, The Rising Sons with Ry Cooder and Taj Mahal, Captain Beefheart and the Magic Band, and Canned Heat, to name a few, the Doors could hardly be expected to hold the title as LA's premier blues rock band, though they left an imprint on blues rock that was uniquely theirs.

With a reliance on the black keys and the blue notes, the Doors' songs favored supernatural minor chords and repeated phrases, the musical and lyrical incantations of blues tradition. And there is nothing more blues than the nighttime – the *mise en scene* of the Doors' song catalog. Morrison's romance with the city of night was a stick poking in the dark corners of consciousness; his myths and tales set between dusk till dawn, the midnight confessions and witching hour magic rituals were borrowed from a blues palette, in all its shades of noir.

Despite their successes, the Doors were living their own version of the blues: Their trials were piling up, largely due to the trouble induced by Jim and his certain lack of control and discipline.

The idea that band life on the road for performing musicians is freewheeling is largely a fantasy: More often, the day is an oddly regimented existence of long drives punctuated by truck stops; it culminates with the performance, and ends in a motel room's unfamiliar bed. The next day is the same, as is the one after that, and a tour can proceed for weeks, or months, through blinding fatigue, tedium, and loneliness that if one is lucky, may be assuaged by a certain mental, physical, and spiritual preparation. There are more rigorous and less fulfilling jobs to be sure, but work is what it implies, and Jim was not one to comply with structure or routine.

Ever since he was a teenager, his father away on military duty, there were few circumstances under which Jim would be told what to do. Certainly in the face of success, there would be no manager or record man whom he'd allow to collar him. If his bandmates were to suggest he get it together, he ignored them. This was a person who slept when he was tired, went to bed wherever and with whomever he felt like sleeping with, showed up when he got there, and left when he was done. He ingested what he needed to get up and to get down, blacked out, and woke up – the essence and mascot of the free loving '60s and living the rock 'n' roll lifestyle.

The beach workouts with Ray had long been abandoned, replaced as they were with business deadlines, rehearsals, gigs, and airport arrival and departure times. Teamwork was a requirement, but the singer was his own man, off and running, and not always prepared for performances and other situations where anything could happen. Problems were developing, and so just as 1967 had ended, 1968 began – with an arrest for Jim Morrison.

Like the cops in New Haven who took a strong dislike to him, in Las Vegas, they didn't like his swagger and the confrontation ended in a beating for Jim. In addition to law enforcement, there were others disdainful of Morrison's misbehavior, including some rock critics and musical peers who were skeptical of his talent and his legitimacy as an artist.

The Jekyll and Hyde-like behavior his friends and drinking associates describe make it safe to say that in all likelihood, Morrison was suffering from the effects of alcoholism, a disease that is partially defined by defiance. An alcoholic of Jim's type was more at one with the universe, more at home and in his own skin, when he was under the influence. Drinking was a part of who he was – an Irishman, a poet, a performer, and a man – and helped to dull the pain of life, from love lost to family disappointment. His deep-seeded anti-authoritarianism, his genealogy, and his soul-searching combined to find him dabbling in various combinations of ingredients, to achieve a perfect sense of wellbeing. And yet one wrong dose of this or that could set him in trouble, turn him into a Frankenstein, or on the path toward self-destruction, as on nights of his bar fights and arrests. Somehow, the unpredictable and dark side of drugs was not enough of a deterrent to using them, perhaps in light of what he was achieving. One illustration of the triumph and tragedy inherent in Jim's substance abuse is the story of "The End." While too much acid and alcohol had resulted in the spontaneous rant that got the band eighty-sixed from its residency at the Whisky, the acid trip had undeniably contributed to the famous Oedipus Rex-inspired section of a song that nearly 50 years after its inception is considered to be one of the finest works in all of rock 'n' roll. Should he have traded the psychedelic experience for a merit badge in good behavior? Hadn't his literary heroes and other artists of note experimented with altered states of consciousness and gotten results? Jim had, in a way, been gifted by his deviance and was being rewarded for it. There were friends who enjoyed the outrageousness, and a press that reveled in reporting on his inebriated antics and alcohol-related weight fluctuations; his girlfriend, by all accounts, shared his appetites. An entire infrastructure had an interest in him maintaining a regular schedule of excess; that is until it didn't: By 1968, in the high era of psychedelics, Jim Morrison's alcohol consumption was peaking. In light of the increased pressure on them professionally, it occurred to the band to ask him to put down the bottle. But stopping was not an option; instead Jim saw it like this: "I think I'm having a nervous breakdown," he told Ray.[3]

The embodiment of Dionysus, the mythological Greek god of wine and theatrics around whom cults had grown, Morrison was now paying the toll for making real that which was meant to be a metaphor for the role of artist in society. The substances no longer working, even his relations with fellow musicians and acquaintances began to sour. He alienated both Jimi Hendrix and Janis Joplin with sexually aggressive behavior; Eric Burdon and Arthur Lee, two renegades who lived well outside laws of social mores and etiquette themselves, complained of Morrison's anti-social behavior, particularly as an uninvited guest in their respective homes.[4] Had he lived and worked in the 21st century, there is no doubt Morrison would be a candidate for a celebrity rehab, or a quiet retreat into a spiritual life of recovery. But the best the Doors could do at the time was to consider a re-evaluation within its ranks.

Using the period between *Strange Days* and the third album, *Waiting for the Sun*, to get its affairs in order, the band continued to tour and to perform locally and began to document its progress on film and with live and studio recordings. Addressing the question of whether to continue to tour under present conditions, with their singer's behavior perpetually rocking them off course, or to turn things around, it was determined the band needed outside assistance. They reconciled their mainstream popularity with their alliance to the underground by hiring a 19-year-old manager, Bill Siddons, and a 13-year-old fan/gopher, Danny Sugarman, youthful staffers in tune with the times. Manzarek was coming up on 30, the age designated by the counterculture as the expiration of one's trustworthiness, and had enough experience to guide the ship: Finding a place at 8512 Santa Monica Boulevard at La Cienega, the Doors set up an office and rehearsal studio/workshop, in the heart of the district where Jim did most of his drinking. The reorganization went someway toward a fresh start; at the very least, people would know where to find Jim.

A Feast of Friends & West Hollywood

Jim Morrison and the California friends he partied with came from all walks of life, though by most accounts, he kept them separate and compartmentalized from each other: Some remember him in one dimension, while others saw both sides of him and more. The coterie from film school, the Venice beach poet's circle, the Hollywood clubbers, record business people, and the women he slept with included but were not limited to: Dennis Jakob, Felix Venable, Alain Ronay, Phil O'Leno, Babe Hill, Tom Baker, Paul Ferrara, Frank Lisciandro, Eve and Mirandi Babitz, Pamela Des Barres, Diane Gardiner, and plenty more. Their on-the-record impressions have contributed to shaping the portrait of Morrison presented here, though it was decided to leave their firsthand accounts to their own books and other projects.

As for the West Hollywood spots still hot from Morrison's repeat visitations, Alta Cienega Motel remains open for business at 1005 N. La Cienega.

Visitors can rent Morrison's old crash pad, Room 32, a must-stay destination for any pilgrim traveler. As an alternative, The Tropicana, formerly at 8585 Santa Monica Blvd, now functions as a Ramada Inn. The original Barney's Beanery at 8447 Santa Monica Blvd. in West Hollywood still stands, serving breakfast all day. A plaque there commemorates one of Morrison's more famous public urination scenes (Barney's had previously been a favorite haunt of Beat-era writers and artists from the Ferus gallery scene). Nearby, Canter's Deli at 419 N. Fairfax remains an all-night diner and rock hangout for musicians and their friends. Family-owned since its founding in LA's Boyle Heights and in its present location since 1953,[5]. Canter's is where, through the years, you could've spotted not only the Doors and Love, but Tom Waits, Rickie Lee Jones, and their pal, Chuck E. Weiss (who has a booth dedicated in his name). In the late '70s/early '80s, it was the place where post-show, punk, and new wave bands would congregate, followed by *Appetite for Destruction*-era Guns and Roses and a '90s crowd that included the Wallflowers, Fiona Apple, and Kanye West producer, Jon Brion. At the turn of the 21st Century, KROQ DJ, Rodney Bingenheimer, and his one-time associate and fellow nightcrawler, Kim Fowley, were still holding a booth for rock 'n' roll at Canter's.

Situated down the hill from the Strip, the Doors' workshop was adjacent to the West Coast headquarters of Elektra Records, 962 North La Cienega Boulevard. The Alta Cienega and Tropicana motels, Morrison's homes away from home, were in the neighborhood, as were two ventures operating at his expense at 947 La Cienega: Pam's bohemian-chic boutique, Themis, and Morrison's HWY film office. With rock 'n' roll watering hole, Barney's Beanery, within spitting distance, the entire area was a crossroads for rock 'n' roll insiders, a thoroughfare for artists, hippies, and music people, seeking a piece of the action. Morrison might take a meal at Players, or he and his gang of drinking buddies would pile into the Phone Booth, a strip joint, and its sister establishment, The Extension, to throw back a few rounds. Sometimes he'd hit the Strip for an after hours breakfast at Ben Frank's or Canter's Deli in Fairfax. Other nights it was Chateau Marmont, 8221 Sunset, a spot where Hollywood types still like to discreetly congregate. He might amble down to Elektra to chat up the assistant promotion staff, then roam the Boulevard, west to The Troubadour, 9081 Santa Monica, where he would inevitably be bounced and ultimately banned. At points further east in Hollywood, like The Kaleidoscope (6230 W. Sunset), he could catch the residency by his friends in Canned Heat, then head back to Elektra, where he would sneak inside, trash someone's office, then sneak out, landing facedown in the building's landscaped border at the end of the night. Other nights he'd drive the roads that snaked into laidback Topanga Canyon, and escape into another side of LA nightlife.

Among the Doors' peers, the artists who dominated '60s rock, most all drank heavily from the deep well of blues inspiration. Bands all over the world riffed on the same songs, rooted in African American history.

As cultural currency, blues-based rock music is like gold, melded and reshaped into whatever it needs to be. Carrying the music forward and bringing it into new dimensions, it can fill a need for a release from oppressive circumstances in the here and now, while also traveling backward in time, conjuring eras when life was more or less sweet for some as it was harsh for others. Up and coming blues players in the '60s studied the phrasing, riffs, and rhymes of Robert Johnson who wrote the book on the modern blues song before he died at age 27. They found out Son House brought his background from preaching, a stay in prison, and did some hard drinking to create a distinct vocal style, accompanied by slide guitar. And everyone knew the Delta's Muddy Waters: the one-time pistol-packing bandleader who moved north and electrified the blues in Chicago, was still alive and laying it down on the rock circuit.

Studying the stories of the songs, their dealings with the supernatural, the frankness of subjects ranging from sex to death, primal fear and family, playing with their mythic tales, magic elixirs, numbers and formulas, were the things the country bluesmen of the early 20th Century did with songs in an effort to transcend circumstance. In some respects, the young kids who studied them were trying to do the same. But had you asked Paul Butterfield, who grew up around the Chicago bluesmen and played with them about the Doors, he would've told you the band didn't have what it takes. "Everyone's trying to play blues these days," he said. "But when a group like the Doors – I'm not singling them out, they just come to mind – tries it, I can't believe them. What they do, they do well. But blues isn't their thing. You've got to have a feeling for the blues."⁵

For better or worse, Morrison, especially, was forever encouraging himself and the band to get back to the roots – the bars and the blues riffs – for their life-sustaining properties. But the Doors needed to reach beyond blues' limits to become what they did; had they persisted with the blues alone, they may've only made it as far as Butterfield's band or Canned Heat.

Canned Heat and the Topanga Scene

Though lacking in original material of the Doors caliber, Canned Heat provided Morrison with a consistent source of inspiration from 1967-1968. Keeping things basic, the band was soaked in blues tradition, and Morrison became a regular at their jams in Topanga Canyon where Canned Heat's co-founder and main songwriter, Al Wilson, and co-founder Bob Hite, also lived. Morrison was utterly taken with the guys' natural vibe, their habit of dressing for stage in work shirts and street clothes, and most notably, with their beards which he eventually adopted. Morrison's mountain man persona is directly attributed to the influence of Canned Heat's performances at Topanga Corral, 2034 N. Topanga Canyon Boulevard, the nightclub that eventually became the inspiration for "Roadhouse Blues." As a largely secret and forgotten influence on Morrison, a bit of the group's history is in order.

Coming from around the Boston folk and blues scene, Al Wilson met Delta bluesman Bukka White during the early '60s folk revival and in short order, White introduced Wilson to another original bluesman, Son House. Working directly with blues legend House, Wilson assisted the singer (who was in decline from alcoholism) in relearning his own songs, and added harmonica to House's 1965 recording session for Columbia. This kind of hands-on torch passing was common during the blues revival as mostly rural, sometimes urban, bluesman taught young whites to play (African American Taj Mahal, mentored by Lightnin' Hopkins in Los Angeles, was the exception to almost every rule). In Boston, Al Wilson was acquainted with another musician/scholar, John Fahey. A folk-guitarist in his own right, Fahey brought Skip "Devil Got My Woman" James out of retirement and learned blues technique from him. Wilson moved to California on Fahey's suggestion, to assist him with finishing the UCLA thesis research he was doing on bluesman Charley Patton. Situated out West, Wilson joined forces with another blues enthusiast, Bob Hite, and with Fahey's friend Henry Vestine, formed a jug band which became Canned Heat, their name taken from an old Tommy Johnson blues. Borrowing their boogie from John Lee Hooker, Canned Heat caught a hit in 1967 with "On the Road Again," merging the moan of the blues with the drone of Indian classical music. Following the success of "On the Road Again," Canned Heat continued to forge their way on the charts, finding an even wider audience for their sound worldwide, particularly in Europe. Another hit, "Going up the Country" (its origins rooted in a 1920s blues), and an appearance at Woodstock, was their peak of mainstream fame in the United States. In addition to bluesology, Al Wilson was an avid environmentalist in the days before there was a movement in place to get back to the land. As

Canned Heat continued to work, Wilson was eventually able to match his love of the land to a concept album, *Future Blues*, and created a foundation to help save the giant redwoods of California. But following just three years of career success, life on the mountain ended for Wilson in 1970 when he died of a barbiturate overdose at the age of 27. His bandmate, Bob Hite, died in 1981.

Topanga Canyon

Rustic and wild, Topanga Canyon provides sanctuary and natural surroundings to LA residents and has historically served as a hideaway for entertainers. Like Venice, it was a coastal getaway for actors in Hollywood's early days. The Chumush tribe named the canyon between Santa Monica and Malibu "Topanga," their word for "above," while Lower Topanga, near the beach, is the tribe's actual sacred land. Communion with nature is the main attraction for the Topanga resident; seclusion and anonymity are also the draws for the creative type who enjoys country living with proximity to the urbanscape.[6]

In the '50s, Woody Guthrie took refuge at Will Geer's ranch high in the hills there. In the mid-'60s, Topanga Corral provided a gig for locals like Canned Heat, blues artists Taj Mahal and Etta James, and laidback proto-jam bands like Spirit and Little Feat. In the '70s, Marvin Gaye and Billy Preston both had homes there, as did various members of the Eagles and Fleetwood Mac. In more recent years, the Black Crowes' Chris

Robinson and freak folk's Devendra Banhart have made associations with Topanga. The Inn of the Seventh Ray, the Topanga Country Store, and Mexican restaurant, Abuelita's, remain popular stop-offs. The Annual Topanga Days Festival on Memorial Day Weekend, as well as the summer performance program at Theatricum Botanicum, on the site of Geer's ranch, are the area's main amusements. What's left of the Topanga Corral, the nightclub that inspired the Doors' "Roadhouse Blues," sits atop the Canyon road. In the back of the roadhouse, there were indeed some bungalows, though they've long been vacated, their memory existing only in the imagination of those who visit there or listen to the song.

Waiting, Waiting....

In February of 1968, a point at which the band could barely imagine continuing for all its internal problems, they began the recording of a third album, *Waiting for the Sun*. Working at TTG Studio in Hollywood, on Sunset and Highland, the studio's 16 tracks, four times as many as on previous Doors records, was perhaps the fresh opportunity they were seeking to inject new life into an old story. Stretching out to experiment, exploring the places hinted at on *Strange Days*, as well as on other highly produced and orchestrated pioneering efforts of the era – the sonic forests planted by the Beach Boys on *Pet Sounds*, the Beatles on *Sgt. Pepper's Lonely Hearts*

Club Band – would be the logical progression for a band with artistic vision and a recording budget in 1968. But production gimmickry didn't inspire the Doors; they were less a studio act than a living and breathing entity. And their schedule off the road didn't allow for them to putter or percolate in preparation to create. Busy working, and working at chasing down Jim, they needed to find simple, organic ways to create, and landed at the intersection of Jim's poetry and the blues, and the band's innate interest in improvisational music.

"Let's talk to Paul about 'Texas Radio' with a little blues accompaniment," Jim said to Ray during a break from the otherwise grueling recording routine. But producer Paul Rothchild didn't have much confidence in what the band could actually achieve. "By the time we hit *Waiting for the Sun* things were getting a little thin,"[7] he said. Scrambling to come up with more material, Rothchild and Morrison culled his notebooks for song ideas, hoping to cobble together pieces and develop whole songs. Thinking back on how his songs took shape, Morrison remarked, "I guess all that time I was unconsciously accumulating inclination and listening. So when it finally happened, my subconscious had prepared the whole thing."[8] Pulling bits from here and scraps of phrases from there, reference upon reference to Mary Werbelow showed up on the pages, providing inspiration for the title song, as well as "Summer's Almost Gone."

"'My Wild Love' is one of those old chain gang songs,"[9] explains Robby Krieger. The chant marries moans of discontent and handclaps to the singer's downbeat lost love lament. "Not to Touch the Earth" was built on a fragment of the "Celebration of the Lizard" poem: The song evolved from Jim's reading of Sir James George Frazier's *The Golden Bough: A Study of Magic and Religion*. Influential upon its publication in 1890, the book has inspired poets, authors, scholars, and philosophers to connect religion and myths in the creation of modern literature.

Some outlaws live by the side of the lake
The minister's daughter's in love with the snake
Who lives in a well by the side of the road
Wake up girl we're almost home

The magic religious tones of "Not To Touch The Earth" conjure the voodoo of Bo Diddley's "Who Do You Love?"

Got a brand new house on the roadside,
made out of rattlesnake hide
I got a brand new chimney made on top,
made out of human skulls
Now come on darlin' let's take a little walk
Tell me who do you love

Diddley's song with its big bad beat, and character with his *cobra snake for a necktie*, developed into a natural cover for the Doors. Jim and Ray had found common ground early on with "Who Do You Love?" while finding their own way toward conjuring some heavy rock'n'blues. Morrison's bond with Bo Diddley was a shared pain, partly subconscious, and locked down tight: His dark night as a boy was reversed when Diddly's "Cracking Up" delivered him from his own private hell. He knew the power of rock 'n' roll poetry and its magical ability to redeem reality, and was attempting to write those kinds of songs. Manzarek also believed in the magic of rock on the radio. "The radio saved my life," he said. "It saved my soul."[10] He too understood the blues and what it meant to the urban dwellers on Maxwell Street, in his sweet home, Chicago. He'd heard the local rock 'n' rollers like Diddley and Chuck Berry, and the blues masters who informed them, Muddy Waters, Howlin' Wolf, and Little Walter, sizzling over the airwaves, sometimes just hours and minutes after the records were cut and pressed by Chess. Diddley had leapt out of his speakers too, capturing his imagination, and the beat was attached to his heart. They wanted to play songs with that kind of juice, too, so they took on Wolf's "Little Red Rooster" and "Back Door Man," the Willie Dixon song to which Kreiger lent his stinging, Waters-like electric tone.

Bo Diddley, Rock 'n' Roll Originator

Bo Diddley was born Ellas Bates in McComb, Mississippi. Relocated at a young age to Chicago and adopted and raised by his mother's McDaniels clan, Ellas was proficient on the violin before he ever picked up a guitar or was rechristened Bo Diddley. As a father of rock 'n' roll, his nickname was the Originator; among his many contributions, he gave the music a distinctive beat, rooted in the African percussive rhythm pattern, *clave*. Diddley was also an innovator on guitar, designing new models and distorting existing ones. Lyrically, his rhymes and themes are off the wall but they cut deep: His insults waged in song, rooted in the African American tradition of the dozens, are forerunners to rap.

One of his earliest sides in a chain of late '50s hit singles was "I'm A Man," his recorded answer to Muddy Waters' "I'm Your Hoochie Coochie Man." The black cat bone and St. John Conqueroo root in that song's lyric are used to make women fall in line under a man's spell, according to voodoo practice. In "Who Do You Love?" Diddley upped the ante, using a rattlesnake whip, tombstone hands, and graveyard mind to drive home his point: "Just 22 and I don't mind dying," he sang. Sometimes bitter, but with a sharp wit and the resilience necessary to survive America, Diddley's music was born in pain, lived in pain, and would die in pain. His was the music that called Jim Morrison into the theater of the blues, with its poetry of courtship and hoodoo, life celebration and laughter in the face of death, and into the arena as a rock 'n' roll performer. Maker of time transcendent music, with the charms and ability to soothe the dangerous mind of the young Jim Morrison, at the time of his death in 2008, Bo Diddley had never really received full payback for his originality and all he gave to rock 'n' roll.

It was becoming clear during the session that Jim's idea to cut "Celebration of the Lizard" was not only an attempt to fill an album side, it was a pipe dream. Following the in-studio collapse of "The Celebration of the Lizard," and the over 100 attempts it took, at Paul Rothchild's insistence, to get "The Unknown Soldier" to his standard of perfection, Morrison entirely lost interest in the recording process; Densmore lost interest in being in the Doors and quit for a time. Rothchild ended up constructing composite vocal tracks from Jim's drunken takes, while other songs were put together off the cuff.

Poured into leather pants and the poet's shirt, the clothes of the Lizard King, the exercise of flipping through his notebooks thrust Morrison into the past amidst an absurd present. A member of a band comprised of people he didn't have much in common with, playing for audiences he didn't much care for, was his reality, when he would've preferred to be pursuing poetry and film, interests that made him feel more alive.

Certainly the film clip for "Unknown Soldier" was a more effective engagement and execution of artistic expression than the studio recording process for it. Featuring the band and Dorothy Fujikawa, Morrison enacts getting shot, a gag he used onstage and had been honing since falling down cold as a kid. Play acting aside, the song and accompanying images of Vietnam combat were a serious attempt at an anti-war statement. The slogan "war is over" and the images of post-war celebration were an affirmation of a future without war. *War is Over (La Guerre Est Finie)* was the title of a 1966 film by Alain Resnais; in his poem "Wichita Vortex Sutra," Allen Ginsberg had posited the idea of declaring an end to the war. Morrison would've been well aware of the works. There was also the Phil Ochs' song, "The War is Over". John Lennon and Yoko Ono turned "war is over, if you want it" into an entire anti-war art campaign and song.

"Five to One," from the same sessions, also concerned war and the military industrial complex, and was sprung from a difficult studio experience. Morrison was ultra-high on a potentially lethal cocktail of alcohol and drugs, and though he didn't pass out, he came close enough, stumbling in on the wrong beat. "But it was such an impassioned performance, we put it on the record anyway,"[11] said Manzarek.

An album that could've held so much potential for experimentation and expansion ended up being viewed as a misstep and a turning point for the band as they moved into a less focused period, exacerbated by their singer's alcohol problem. It was suggested that as a way to keep Jim on track, a companion could be called in to assist. Visual artist and singer-songwriter Bob Neuwirth was hired under the pretense of making a *cinéma vérité* film, with the implicit instruction to keep one eye on Jim. The idea of anyone controlling Jim was a non-starter, though a film was completed—a clip to accompany the dreamlike, "Not to Touch the Earth." Despite the obstacles, film remained a consistent force and exerted a positive influence on Morrison, if not a source of intrigue for him and his friends. The establishment of a film production company, HWY, facilitated the launch of the film, *Feast of Friends*, shot at the Doors expense. Though he'd been offered outside movie roles by directors (including Andy Warhol who had hoped to cast a nude Jim in one of his films), it was not to be: Morrison, intending to star in his own film, had little time for Hollywood and was entirely put-off by the Warhol superstar scene at the Factory (though he did take inspiration from the hell for leather act by the Plastic Exploding Inevitable dancer, Gerard Malanga). Jim immediately ordered "leathers" of his own design, in snakeskin – the first of their kind with jeans-styling – inspired by Xavier Valentine's jacket, as worn by Marlon Brando in *The Fugitive Kind*.

Runnin' Blue

Morrison and the Doors were living in California style: forming their own production companies, driving cool cars, ordering bespoke clothes, loving the ladies of the canyon, and living with bohemian style in hippie-haven homes. But for all his notoriety, charisma, and ostensible success, Jim continued to prefer other people's couches and flophouses; he had very little to show for his achievements beyond the snakeskin pants which, according to some reports, he wouldn't shed for days on end. Continuing to record on and off with stops and starts for performances – to which Jim showed up in varying degrees of drunk and soberness throughout the spring – where the Doors went, trouble followed.

Shows were becoming increasingly erratic: There were nights when critics wrote them off as buffoons, while on other nights they mesmerized, and audiences responded accordingly. The crowd got their money's worth the night the Doors topped a bill featuring Bo Diddley, Traffic, and Canned Heat at the Kaleidoscope, a benefit concert for the striking workers of Pasadena City College radio station KPCC. But in Chicago, Morrison worked up the audience into such a negative state they stormed the stage, forcing the band's quick exit through a side door. The lackluster attention at an afternoon gig in Santa Clara, Northern California, was blamed on the daylight (and Jim's newly shorn locks which reportedly received more notice than the music). Despite the unpredictability, they filled large halls and arenas, commanded some of the highest performance fees a band could receive (reportedly clearing five figures), and it was all being preserved and recorded, in preparation for the live album.

Producer Paul Rothchild knew he had his hands full and was generally fed up with the process, but also seemed to understand where Morrison was trying to go with his guises as poet, bluesman, and Lizard King, "a character that Jim seemed to actively create and manipulate in his exploration of the human soul.... He created these personae to explore places you and I wouldn't go."[12] Rothchild described the role of a shaman – someone who mediates between the earthly and spirit worlds – an explorer of places un-navigable by the average traveler.

"I've read a little about shamanism, but I haven't seen much of it firsthand," Morrison once said. "But in tribes, a shaman can be any age, and the whole tribe, all ages, kinda push him into his trip and listen to him," he said. "I don't think the shaman from what I've read is really too interested in defining his role in society, he's really more interested in pursuing his own fantasies."[13]

Welcome to the Soft Parade

Released in July, *Waiting for the Sun* was not well received in the marketplace and the band immediately took to the newly completed Elektra Sound Recorders for the making of *The Soft Parade*. The Doors' fourth album is widely remembered for its kitchen sink approach to rock, but from its blue-toned cover to its entire repertoire, the album is, in fact, kind of blue. Featuring the surreal rocker, "Shaman's Blues" as well as the tribute to Otis Redding, "Runnin' Blue," and a title cut that kicks out the jams for a big rock 'n' roll finish, there are also hints of the old, garage-blues inspired days of the band. Shapeshifting and ranting, it is melodically and lyrically surprising throughout. Krieger nailed the most accessible songs, "Touch Me," "Tell All the People" and "Wishful Sinful." Morrison's songs, "Shaman's Blues," "Wild Child" and "The Soft Parade," among them, painted more far-out pictures, accompanied by jams developed by the band.

"When we used to play in clubs, over half of what we did was blues," said Morrison. "We used our own material on records. The most exciting things we did were basic blues things. I like them because they're fun to sing. We may do a few old ones, but we're basically doing original blues, if there is such a thing."

"It starts out with a rhythm, and you don't know how it's going to end up, or how long it's going to be, or really what it's about, until it's over. That sort I enjoy best," Morrison told *Rolling Stone*, a few years down the road. "I guess I'm referring to a blues thing. I get a rhythm, a river of sound rolling along, and I can just completely relax and not worry about time, or how it's going to begin or end or what I'm going to say. But not all people enjoy listening to that."[14]

With enough self-awareness to know he was no master of

the form, and that the elongated blues jam was not every music fan's idea of a good time, Morrison nevertheless thought more and more of creating rambling songs. Densmore wasn't at all a fan of the blues jam; Krieger's preferences were "more complex," a reflection of the guitarist's fusion of Spanish and Indian classical motifs with blues-based licks. Krieger had a feeling for the music (he'd brought to the table Willie Dixon's "Back Door Man" which he learned from John Hammond Jr.'s version; he knew how to hammer his notes in blues style, and took his inspiration for the refrain "follow me down" in "Tell All the People" from "Fannin Street" by Lead Belly). He was uninterested in straight-up interpretations and preferred to disguise the source of his inspiration. Because of the schism in song styles, *The Soft Parade* marks the point at which the Doors receive individual credit for songs rather than the usual collective. Generally speaking, Morrison's contributions to the album are largely the unembellished and blues-based tracks while Krieger's are the more ambitious and layered compositions.

"The person who writes the songs ought to sing them because he's the one that can feel it more than anyone else," said Morrison. "Since I was writing the songs, I gradually became a singer."[15]

Attempting to split this difference on *The Soft Parade*, Jim and Robby's voices merged on "Runnin' Blue," their tribute to Otis Redding. Referencing his album *Otis Blue*, "Runnin' Blue" begins with rewritten lines from the Lead Belly song, "Poor Howard:" *Poor Otis been and gone*. Jim sings of needing to get back to LA and "the dock of the bay," another nod to Redding, while Jim and Ray's own meetings on Venice beach were actually at the edge of

Santa Monica Bay (the nearest docks are at LA's port cities, San Pedro and Long Beach). The song also features a strange juxtaposition between old-time fiddle music and orchestrated soul, a bit like a mash-up or sound collage (the pastiche pre-dates sampling by about 15 years). It was an effective "discombulation," but as a song, it's a failure.

Certainly "Runnin' Blue" is nostalgic for a time when life was simpler for the Doors. Getting back to the bay and the old time sound, would mean turning back time, toward the era of early rock 'n' roll when rhythm and blues was first married to country sound. It was a time when the band from Venice still played barrooms and dances, and one of the kings of rock 'n' soul, Otis Redding, still held down the stage at the Whisky A Go Go.

Lead Belly and Otis Redding

American folk and blues singer Lead Belly is the great, lost influence on rock 'n' roll. His complete recordings were issued in 1966 by the Doors' record label, Elektra, which may account for his apparent ghost on The Soft Parade tracks, "Tell All the People" and "Runnin' Blue." But long before and well after the Doors' attempts to infuse their music with his authentic Louisiana blues, rooted in Southern chain gang songs and strife, Lead Belly would impact popular musicians as diverse as Woody Guthrie, Odetta, and Kurt Cobain.

Soul singer Otis Redding was in a league with Wilson Pickett, James Brown, Sam Cooke, and

Solomon Burke. Raised in Macon, Georgia, Redding first found success on the so-called Chitlin' Circuit, and then became a giant of soul music, owing to his strong emotional voice and epic repertoire that included "I've Been Loving You Too Long," "Respect," and "Try a Little Tenderness." Success in Europe and on rock 'n' roll stages like the Fillmore in the US, translated into further mass appeal following his appearance at Monterey Pop in 1967. Though reaching a wide cross section of people, and larger and larger audiences, by the end of the year, the music world was shattered by his death in a tragic and mysterious plane crash that ended his life prematurely at age 26.

In August of 1968, following a concert at Long Island's Singer Bowl, 200 concertgoers ended the Doors' show by destroying the venue's seating and rushing the stage; once the crowd started demolishing the equipment, the Doors were forced to quickly exit stage left. The responses Morrison had hoped he could provoke by his performances were the exact kind of reactions law enforcement was sent in to control: Three in attendance were taken to the hospital for injuries and two of them were arrested. The band's European concert appearances that summer with Jefferson Airplane and Canned Heat were similarly erratic and potentially dangerous.

On a stopover in London, Morrison paid a visit to the Beatles, in the studio recording their white album, its songs composed during their trip to India with the Maharishi earlier in the year. He hung out with San Francisco Beat writer Michael McClure whose overseas trip coincided with Jim's. The two poets shared any number of intersecting interests, including mind expanding peyote visions and Artaud's Theater of Cruelty. McClure was part of the community of artists associated with Wallace Berman, which also included Morrison's old UCLA instructor, Jack Hirschman, among other poets, visual artists, and writers, who provided a link between the West Coast Beat and hippie generations. It was during their initial meeting that McClure encouraged Morrison's writing and suggested his poems could be published.

Upon returning to the US in October to continue recording *The Soft Parade*, the Doors put in a string of uneven performances. In Phoenix the band was banned for life following a near riot between crowd and security, incited by Morrison. They disappointed the largest crowd ever assembled to see them at LA's massive Forum by debuting material from their unreleased album in progress, and then ultimately delighted fans nationwide with their appearance on the *Smothers Brothers Comedy Hour*.

Wild Child

"Our next guests have a sound that's a very fine sound and more than that, they have the ability to combine that sound with their very own poetry," said Tom Smothers, by way of introduction to "Wild Child," a new song that emerged during *The Soft Parade* sessions.

An ancient lunatic reigns
In the trees of the night

"Wild Child" would become yet another nickname to add to Morrison's list of alter-egos, from the Lizard King to Mr. Mojo Risin', but the back story on this alternate sobriquet is often overlooked: The original *enfant sauvage*, Victor of Aveyron, was a real boy, discovered in the woods in Saint-Sernin-Sur-Rance in the late 1700s. More commonly known as the Wild Boy of Aveyron (the 1970 Truffaut film *Wild Child*, also concerns the Victor of Aveyron story), the feral child is a theme in French arts and culture, and is coincident with Morrison's study of the literature of the Age of Enlightenment.

Jean Marc Gaspar Itard was a young doctor whose work with Victor of Aveyron forged the beginnings of education for the hearing-impaired, and ways of educating mentally and physically disabled children. Itard asserted that language and empathy are the defining characteristics of human life, an idea that dovetailed with advances in human understanding during the Enlightenment. Victor of Aveyron was frequently used as an example in the debates concerning what distinguished man from other animals.[16] It's easy to make the leap from the interests of philosophers, Rousseau and Voltaire, Descartes, Locke, and their dialogues on civility, to Morrison's interest in their philosophies, and specifically the case of Victor. If civility generally means to be reasonable and understanding, then to perceive the plight of the wild child without compassion is to be uncivil or cruel.

The Smothers Brothers also served as the forum to perform the band's latest single, "Touch Me." "We had turned down a lot of TV shows," explained Densmore. "We felt TV kinda mediocritized everything." After a failed lip-synch appearance on teen-music series *Where the Action Is*, it was easy to understand why the Doors would be leery of television. But the Smothers show represented something different: The comedians were personally aligned with left-wing politics. "I remember the audience kinda were scared of us," recalled Densmore.

"Touch Me" was also the fulfillment of the band's dream to work jazz into their sound. "Before we even started, we'd talked about jazz and wanting to expand our sound and experiment. Curtis Amy is playing saxophone on the end of 'Touch Me,'" said Densmore. "We'd lost our innocence; there's horns and strings on 'Touch Me' which we got criticized for. It was number one but the critics put us down." Perhaps it was the meant-to-be-comedic "stronger than dirt" coda borrowed directly from an Ajax commercial that rubbed them wrong....

While attempting to bring the *Soft Parade* project to completion in 1968, Morrison began to lay down a conceptual piece he was calling "Rock is Dead." Mayhem predictably ruled the studio session, and drinking and drug taking inevitably escalated; the period culminated with another driving under the influence [DUI] arrest for Morrison in LA. Though chaos was largely the order of the day inside and outside the studio, before the sessions ended, the Doors captured with swinging jazz-blues tension, Morrison's between-two-worlds dilemma in "Shaman's Blues."

There will never be another one like you
There will never be another one who can do the things you do
Will you give another chance?
Will you try a little try?

Trying to reach Mary Werbelow, he'd asked her once, "Don't you know, the first three albums are about you?"[17] But Mary had not heard a note of the Doors, not since she and Jim parted. By the end of 1968, there was little chance that she would again hear him calling her from the radio or a record player: Traveling in India, seeking to connect with what she'd lost in Los Angeles, the increased distance between them left Jim haunted by his memories and alone, under the big black sun.

Can you give me sanctuary?
I must find a place to hide
A place for me to hide

Lost in the world, reckoning with adulthood, striving to be heard and to make a difference, an entire generation of wild children were at a crossroads: While their concerns for equality among races and genders, free speech against the war, and protections for the environment had shaken up the '60s, the world was moving rapidly in a fresh direction. The societal and political movements brought to light, the striving for reason and civility, would largely come undone by the 21st Century, the eventualities of warning bells left unheeded. Who could have predicted reason alongside compassion for those less fortunate would be at a premium, that healthcare and shelter would become so costly and complicated? Or that ongoing war, mass incarceration, global economic devastation, and ecological disaster, inspired by corporate and consumer greed, would await? This is the real apocalyptic nightmare, its conditions foretold by Morrison and his fellow travelers, out on the perimeter.

CHAPTER 6

Paradise Lost: 1969

Recording continued but was not going well on the extended sessions for *The Soft Parade*, while the downward spiral that characterized Jim's drinking in 1968 grew to problematic proportions in 1969. Starting the year with an arrest (driving without a license/DUI) in Los Angeles, the further charges of public drunkenness on March 1, 1969 in Miami were indisputable. But it was the pending inquiry into Jim's alleged obscene behavior there that would pull the band into a compromised state for the entire year, if not the rest of its days. Long considered to be the pivotal event in the Doors' career, "The Miami Incident" is better understood through the events preceding it as well as through the culture of a time when free speech was persistently put on trial.

For his part, Morrison was very, very drunk that night; not that he needed an excuse, a series of delayed flights and airport lounge layovers contributed to his excessive drinking with intent. And though he personally had little recollection of what happened at the Dinner Keys Auditorium in Coconut Grove, it was crystal clear that being brought to trial meant he was not only being used as a pawn in a political game, but that artistic freedom was at stake. "In the realm of art and theater, there should be complete freedom for the artist and perfomer," he said in his own defense.[1]

Morrison knew not only free speech precedents but the history of performance and the power in the ritual of it. With an authority vested in his belief in the artist's function to provoke responses from the audience, his themes complimented the youth movement's desire to break free from cultural norms and constrictions.

Preceding World War I, the arts and literature were consumed with apocalyptic visions –the rivers of blood, primed to cover the world. Just as the artist/poet/philosophers of the early 20th Century had reckoned with America's new superpower, rooted in industry and domination, time has revealed that Morrison was working during a particularly dark period in America's political history. Channeling and grappling with similar dark truths in the '60s, his duality as a shaman made him a psychic culvert as well as a scapegoat, but he wasn't going to go down without a fight. He understood an artist's public life had a double edge; he had known of artistic witch-hunts and obscenity trials. He remembered firsthand the Bay Area and national coverage of Allen Ginsberg's and Lawrence Ferlinghetti's victory with *Howl*. Encouraged by the poet Michael McClure, he was further fuelled by the dramatic story and styles of the Living Theater.

A Theater Trip

Founded by Julian Beck and Judith Malina, the Living Theater company practiced a confrontational style of drama featuring audience interaction, and no division between life and art. The troupe's plays were intended to awaken the spirit of the art of theater, moving it away from entertainment and more toward rousing and challenging audiences. With performances that resulted in chaos unique to the usually staid theater environment, their manifesto states: "The purpose of the play is to lead to a state of being in which non-violent revolutionary action is possible." Returning to the states from Europe, following a self-imposed exile, the Living Theater performed *Paradise Now* in Los Angeles and San Francisco in early 1969. Crowd participation in the production was encouraged, and Morrison was taken with the idea: He attended the Living Theater's Los Angeles performances for four nights running at USC's Bovard Auditorium, as well as a performance at Nourse Auditorium in San Francisco where he and McClure joined the actors onstage.

The group had been around since 1947, staging poetic dramas by Gertrude Stein and John Ashbery, and hosting work by European masters like Lorca and Brecht; the Living Theater is also credited for starting the off-Broadway theater scene. Staging works associated with writers from Jean Genet to Jack Kerouac, Morrison had a familiarity with the works and knew well that the radical performance group operated at risk: The company was routinely shut-down in a fury by authorities for obscenity, as well as for spurious code and IRS violations. It spent much of the '60s performing in makeshift spaces after ousters from one venue after another.

In 1965, following one such closure, experimental film director Jonas Mekas surreptitiously filmed a final Living Theater production of the Kenneth H. Brown play, *The Brig*, a statement on the inhumanity of the penal system. Mekas' guerilla film approach, and the Living Theater's participation in it, was yet another validation to Morrison: As he'd suspected when he had the impulse to join the Mekas film collective after graduation from UCLA, these artists were his kind of people and he belonged on the continuum of libertine art. Morrison made at least one known donation to the Living Theater and Beck, who were not profit-motivated, and as a result, were financially hard pressed.[2]

The Living Theater's California performances marked the beginning of the end of the Doors as they were known; without a doubt it was a turning point for Morrison, away from the rock 'n' roll circus and into the more demanding realm of political and social theater. A couple of years after witnessing the watershed theatrical performances, Morrison told *Rolling Stone*, "It took me awhile to realize that this thing – performing rock and roll songs – was really about a theater trip. That's when I understood what was going on." Conjoining his experience with the Living Theater, with the spirits of the blues and outlaw poetry, Morrison knew he was conjuring a primal and instinctual contemporary rock 'n' roll. Casting spells with the music, creating impenetrable codes to those outside the counterculture, he began smashing perceptions, destroying myths, and breaking through to other dimensions in surrealist, theatrical technique. Antonin Artaud had explored such an approach with the Theater of Cruelty; Morrison was practicing his own version of living rock 'n' roll theater.

Awakening audiences to revolutionary ideas, feelings, and actions, pointing toward new directions and paradigms beyond mop tops, mod-suits, flower power, and psychedelia, Morrison's nightly ceremonies with audiences and visionary poetry recitations were attempts to shine a light into reality's dark corners. The ecstatic nature of the performance, the shamanistic reliance on animal powers – the lizards and snakes – and the surrealistic impulse to rearrange the senses in an effort to break through to new realities, were Morrison's means to imparting his message to a world in peril.

But the addition of alcohol into the already heady mix generally ended in catastrophe. Four days after the show at the Dinner Key Auditorium in Coconut Grove, Miami, the Dade County Sheriff issued a warrant for Morrison's arrest: He was charged on a felony count for lewd and lascivious behavior, and the misdemeanor crimes of public drunkenness, profanity, and indecent exposure. None of the Doors would recollect anything indecent about the performance, though the facts remain: Morrison arrived at the gig drunk. Perhaps most unusual for a Doors show was the appearance of a live lamb, brought to the stage (a gift from a militant vegan, Lewis Marvin). He riled the crowd with verbal assaults ("How long are you going to let them push you around? Maybe you like it. Maybe you love it...You're all a bunch of slaves...What are you gonna do about it? What are you gonna do?"). Somewhere in this mix was Mary, Jim repeating the repetitive refrain *"India, India, India, India..."* during his onstage undoing in Miami. Turning in a sloppy performance spiced with more invective rant, he threatened to expose himself. A month of cancelled tour dates followed, and by April 3, Morrison had turned himself in to the Los Angeles office of the FBI. Pleading not guilty in the fall, the trial was still nine months away and remained very much on everyone's mind.

Later Jim would reportedly joke with friends and Pamela Courson that he dropped his pants onstage, though no evidence of his exposure was ever produced. When called on to address the matter publicly, Morrison always recounted in concrete and clear-headed terms, a night that appeared to be a set-up for his arrest, but the event and pressure of the impending trial took Jim on a bender that some would say lasted for the remainder of his life.

No longer able to contain their misery with him, in spring of 1969, the band called a meeting with the purpose of confronting their singer, much in the way a modern intervention would be conducted today. "You're killing yourself," Manzarek told Morrison. "The booze is killing your spirit." "I know I drink too much," he said. "I'm trying to quit."[3]

While his Scottish-Irish heritage and genetics likely played a role in Morrison's predisposition toward alcoholism, there appears to have been an equal measure of family dysfunction and other environmental factors that contributed to his affliction. From as far back as anyone who knew him could remember, a couple of drinks awakened the beast in an otherwise good natured and sober Jim. The invisible line between alcoholic and normal drinker is difficult to delineate and partly why alcoholism is termed a self-diagnosed disease; recovery from alcoholism requires acknowledgment of defeat by the drinker, and Morrison had not reached a level of admittance. But it's safe to say that rarely does the non-alcoholic drinker find cause to urinate in public places or to deliver semi-regular rants, charged with racial epithets on the regular, the way Morrison did while under-the-influence. These repellent, alcohol-induced sprees horrified observers who claim to have witnessed them, people who otherwise knew Jim to be a decent person. The Doors called this version of Morrison Jimbo, his nature vulgar, belligerent, and violent. This super-human inebriate could emerge from death-defying situations unscathed, while on other occasions he might land face down in the gutter. He might not remember any of it, but was only too happy to repeat the offending behaviors over and over again, a pattern characteristic of alcoholism.

Densmore, Kreiger, and Manzarek did not appear to suffer from the disease of alcoholism themselves, but like beleaguered spouses, they were bothered by Jim's drinking, not only when it reared its head professionally, but personally. "You see, he wanted drinking buddies and the Doors just wouldn't drink together," wrote Ray. Tending to their own spirits with meditation, the ancient practice that slows the breath and quiets the mind, they coped with the inevitable ups and downs of life with an alcoholic, though there is little evidence to support they understood anything about his disease or the way it impacted their band, as it would a family. The following may assist in a greater understanding of the condition of alcoholism, how it affected Jim Morrison, and the toll it took on the collective energies of the Doors.

Alcoholism, Archetypes, Carl Jung and the Collective Unconscious

Alcoholics Anonymous, founded in 1939 on the principle of one alcoholic helping another to recover from alcoholism, was certainly active in the 1960s, but it was not a place where Morrison or anyone in the Doors organization considered turning for help. Manzarek says, "That was for old winos and left-over Fifties rummies. Strictly skid row and *Days of Wine and Roses* types. We were on our own."

"On a very basic level, I love drinking," Morrison told *Rolling Stone* in 1969. "But I can't see drinking just milk or water or Coca Cola. It just ruins it for me. You have to have wine or beer to complete a meal," he said. "Getting drunk…you're in complete control up to a point. It's your choice, every time you take a sip. You have a lot of small choices. It's like….I guess it's the difference between suicide and slow capitulation." Asked what it all means, he replied, "I don't know man. Let's go next door and get a drink."

The great analyst Carl Jung was a man who also lived by his own code and philosophies, writing the script for his self-styled experiments and enacting his own fantasies. Studying his dreams and developing his theories on archetypes and the collective unconscious in the theater of his mind, it is generally understood that the period in which Jung conducted his research on the unconscious, he was perceived to be having a psychotic break – a common diagnosis of visionaries and thinkers on the leading edge. Nevertheless, Jung's intent concentration on his work brought forth valuable theories on collective unconscious, individuation, and archetypes, still in circulation today. A modern world in which we had none of Jung's reports of his attempts to "get in touch with his own myth," or the findings from his studies of his own dreams and visions (in which he was often visited by a large black snake), would change the framework for viewing so many of our own experiences.

What would Jung have made of Morrison? What conclusions might he have drawn based on Jim's condition and the shapes of his mind, his performance aesthetic, and the idea that he likely suffered from alcoholism? Perhaps if Morrison's own experiments with the unconscious, his inspiration to take LSD fired by Aldous Huxley's reports on mescaline, and his own primordial image of a Lizard King were viewed through a Jungian lens, he would be seen less as an abusive, substance addicted madman and more of a seer – with prophetic messages containing valuable information that can help us today. Certainly the deep well he tapped goes some way toward explaining why listeners return to Morrison and the Doors' work on a consistent basis, nearly 50 years after it was created, when other material from the era has been buried or tossed away.

Jung's work in mystical realms contributes to his standing as a somewhat polarizing figure in psychoanalysis. It is also perhaps relevant to note that it was Jung who first equated man's thirst for alcohol as "the equivalent on a low level of the spiritual thirst of our being, expressed in mediaeval language: the Union with God."[4]

It has been noted by scholars who specialize in cultural shifts that the '60s generation's collective seeking was in part based on a thirst for knowledge beyond what was offered at an institutional level. As Allen Ginsberg put it, "But there has been no recognition of this insight on the part of the fathers and teachers (Father Zossima's famous cry!) of these young. What's lacking in the great institutions of learning? The specific wisdom discipline that the young propose: search into inner space."[5]

Eastern mysticism, acid trips, and peyote rituals were all perceived as paths to enlightenment in the psychedelic era. But to "ride the snake," whether meaning to take a LSD trip, to develop a sense of self-awareness below the surface, or something else entirely, could be dangerous business for those inflicted with alcoholism and addictions. In a letter to Bill Wilson, founder of Alcoholic's Anonymous, Jung wrote, "You see, you use the same word for the highest religious experience, as well as for the most depraving poison. The helpful formula therefore is: *spiritum contra spiritus* or a spiritual connection to counter the connection to spirits."[6]

In the mid-'60s, the years Morrison's substance use was peaking, there was still little known in medical science terms about the long-term effects of drug and alcohol abuse, though Jung's work was a beginning toward understanding what drives the alcoholic mind – to attention, to perfection, and self-hatred. Though the American Medical Association has classified alcoholism as a disease, the condition remains one of life's mysteries: Why should alcohol's deleterious effects impact some so harshly, while others may imbibe and remain safe from personality conflicts and loss of bodily control? There are of course those who abstain entirely or are completely ambivalent about the stuff. Doctors generally agree that family history can play a role, as does childhood abuse or trauma, but all consensus departs on matters of the disease as a psychiatric disorder with a mental illness component, or whether it's a matter of "willpower and strength of character".

By 2012, *Alcoholics Anonymous* was listed by the Library of Congress, between Thornton Wilder's *Our Town* and John Steinbeck's *The Grapes of Wrath*, among the 88 Books That Shaped America. Had Jim Morrison the occasion to read it or walk through the door of an AA meeting, it may've helped him discover the relief known to alcoholics who adhere to its program. Alcoholism by AA's definition is an allergy of the body, an obsession of the mind and a malady of the spirit – a threefold disease. By putting down the drink and by retraining thought patterns to stay focused on the present instead of the future or the past, alcoholism is arrested; by feeding the spirit – not in a codified or religious way, but by developing a relationship to a higher consciousness or power that feels right to the alcoholic – alcoholism is treatable.

The Cult of Dionysus

Though he'd clearly crossed the invisible line from casual use into addiction and alcoholism, Morrison's drunken revelries and so-called morbid preoccupations were not entirely uncalculated. The Dionysian Mysteries, ancient Greek and Roman rituals in which wine and music played a role in unleashing inhibitions, was very much a part of the rising awareness and consciousness of the '60s. Alongside Eastern religion and philosophy, the young generation sought to upend patriarchal systems of oppression and to smash outmoded aspects of Judeo-Christian dogma through drug experimentation, astrology, and the occult, and occasionally looked to the gods, goddesses, and myths of Greece and Rome for inspiration. One of the key texts contributing to a greater understanding of the nature of ritual, and the role of the arts, specifically poetry, in transcendence and transformation was *The White Goddess* by Robert Graves. Writing on mushroom cults and tripartite goddess worship, he ignited the imaginations of poets and artists, taking readers into realms beyond George Frazer's *The Golden Bough*, the original text devoted to the intersection at magic and religion.

At the time of Morrison's exploration into alternative paths to enlightenment, there was a growing and general awareness among youth culture that death was "as American as cherry pie," according to the widely circulated quote by activist H. Rap Brown. The idea that the founding of America wasn't exactly clean and virtuous was beginning to penetrate the consciousness of so-called good Americans. There was more of a collective willingness to speak of the slaughter of the indigenous people and ancients of California, of the increasing numbers of young draftee soldiers in body bags, returning home from Vietnam, and of their non-combatant casualties, the innocent citizens in Southeast Asia caught in the crosshairs of war. By recounting and foreshadowing the wars of aggression that disrupt the fragile balance of the earth, Morrison's archetypal motifs, his descriptions of events and images, and his creation of mythical figures aligned him with a tradition among artists since Athenian times who coped with outer realities of the world through artistic expression and revelry. And while he may not have employed the usual tools of the shaman, the divining rods and occult oracles of the ancient world, he used his life and platform as a modern performing artist to speak truth: 50 years later some of his ideas would still be decried as *esoteric* or *alternative* knowledge (climate change denial as an example).

While a wide segment of people in the '60s were responding to cultural agitation, acknowledging the old ways of thinking were outmoded and opening to new areas of study, there were also entire regions of the US unmoved by the shift in consciousness: A conservative backlash and refreshed local and federal agendas toward law and order would find artists like the Doors facing cancellations and other harassments, especially in the post-Miami heat.

In the unscheduled gaps, Morrison was granted more time to pursue his other interests: He worked on *HWY*, the experimental film made by his friends Babe Hill, Frank Lisciandro, and Paul Ferrara, starring Jim as a lone hitchhiker. Loosely based on Morrison's experiences in Florida, thumbing it home to Mary, the 50-minute film was made on location in the California desert near Palm Springs (an untraditional screenplay survives as the poem *HWY: An American Pastoral*). Shot partly in the native land of the Agua Caliente Cahuilla Indians, Tahquitz Canyon (named after an Indian chief with shamanistic powers) and its falls, the surviving film clips of Morrison swimming, hiking, and driving on the desert are taken from the shoot, though the film rarely screens in its entirety. "Essentially there's no plot, no story in the traditional sense. A person comes down from the mountains and hitchhikes his way into a modern city which happens to be LA,"[7] explained Morrison.

In the spring of 1969, *Feast of Friends*, Ferrara's film portraying life on the road from a band's eye view, screened at the Cinematheque 16 on Sunset Strip. Staged as a benefit to raise money for the New York mayoral campaign of Norman Mailer, who had long been one of Morrison's favorite writers, the program was rounded out with the Andy Warhol film, *I a Man*, and poetry readings by Michael McClure and Morrison, who read *An American Prayer*, accompanied by Robby. Though he supported the author's bid for mayor, Morrison decided against going East to campaign for Mailer. "I would have liked to have helped... but I don't believe it would've helped anyone much, my being there." He told *Rolling Stone*, "I'm not any more interested in the mechanics of political operation than I am in the space shot or microbiology or anything else. It's just one thing I know almost nothing about in a practical sense."

In a *Feast of Friends* outtake, Morrison speaks with a minister who appears to be an ardent fan and supporter of the Doors and their anti-war stance: It is a significant statement in a generally high season of attacks on the counter-culture, where even in freaky California, a right-wing siege was progressing. On the same page of the July 12 edition of *Rolling Stone* that designated Doors correspondent Jerry Hopkins recounted the Cinematheque 16 event, reporter Ben Fong-Torres wrote on the California Board of Education's receipt of a report from a concerned conservative citizens group and their proposal to return "moral instruction" to California public schools. Basing their teachings on a combination of wisdom culled from the founding fathers, the Navy, the Marine Corps, and the Bible, with aims to "restore morality among kids," and to correct rampant drug use, sexual freedom and violence, "No mention was made, curiously enough, on the evils of nicotine, Miltowns, alcohol, air pollution, wife-swapping, illegitimate war caused deaths and police violence,"[8] wrote Fong-Torres. The proposed program never made it past the planning or public hearing phase, though it is an illustration of what the counter-culture was up against in freethinking California, and illuminates the role of the state's then-governor, Ronald Reagan, who went on to lead the United States in its broader flight to the right. The alternative press and rock 'n' roll did what it could to stem the tide of the moral majority, as students and youth around the world continued to wage wars against the systems that oppressed them. But throughout the '60s, governments in the US and outside it fought back with counter-intelligence and covert military operations of their own: These counter-attacks are as much a hallmark of the decade as were the people's cries for peace and love.

Just a year after the student massacre at the time of the Mexico Olympics in 1968, the Doors played in Mexico where they were beloved.[9] "That place is a hotbed of political unrest... I heard some stories down there that would curl your hair," Morrison told interviewer Howard Smith. "Dig this: These guys are going to school, you know, college. If one of their friends disappears, they don't see him for like two weeks, they just write him off they say 'well, I guess they got him.' When we went down there, it was the first anniversary of a year earlier... it's when the Olympics were going on... when the students showed up for the protest, there was an ambush waiting and I think they slaughtered about 2,000 young students...

Of course that's just hearsay. I can't back that up with any photographs, but that's what I heard."[10] Eventually, public records revealed government-employed snipers massacred students and bystanders in Tlatelolco.

Robby Krieger told the *Village Voice* he also found the European audiences to be politically motivated. "If we said anything political, they'd go into a furor – they'd love it – especially anything against America. They really dug the political side of it. In America, it's really just the opposite. I think they come more for the religious experience."[11]

"I think rock concerts have always served a function," said Morrison. "It gives a lot of people with the same station in life a chance to gather together and assemble and just feel the sheer mass of them that exists."

The desire for a collective, communal experience was of course exemplified by the event of the season in the summer of '69: Woodstock. The Doors famously did not perform there; Jim and *Feast of Friends* were on the film festival circuit, between the Doors fulfilling their tour dates – that is, when they weren't being cancelled.

When *The Soft Parade* was released in July, Morrison wasn't especially pleased with the album as a whole. "It kinda got outta control… An album, like a book of stories, should have some kind of theme or unified feeling or style about it…" he said. Neither did *Rolling Stone* care much for the album, suggesting such alternate titles as *The Worst of The Doors, Kick Out The Doors*, and *The Soft Touch*, and went as far as to say it was "sad." "It's sad because one of the most potentially moving forces in rock has allowed itself to degenerate," said writer Alec Dubro in his August 23, 1969 review. Referring to the orchestration as "the most cliché ridden sounds, this side of 101 Strings," and Morrison's crooning comparable to square vocalists like Jerry Vale and Andy Williams, the final blow crashed down: "The Doors appear to be in the final stages of musical constipation."

To be sure *The Soft Parade* was a mixed bag, though time has shown the title cut to be an epic showcase for all the elements Jim worked with, from the poetry of William Blake and T.S. Elliott from his youth, to his blues fascination and invitation to "meet me at the crossroads outside of town." Performing "The Soft Parade" in 1969 on the PBS show Critique, Morrison became reacquainted with writer Patricia Kennealy, one of a handful of prolific female music journalists at the time and a hard critic of his poetry. As one of the few who very much liked "The Soft Parade," her positive reception encouraged Jim's marriage of mind/body/spirit through artistic expression.

"Jim always said he knew when something came to him whether it would be a song or a poem, and not just because one showed up with music and the other didn't,"[12] remembered Kennealy.

Following the middling reception of *The Soft Parade* the band seriously considered the direction for its next project. "The initial flash is over," said Morrison plainly. "The thing they call rock, what used to be called rock and roll – it got decadent… it became self-conscious, which I think is the death of any moment. The energy is gone. There is no longer a belief." Morrison's trials on the road, the poor reviews of *Waiting for the Sun* and *The Soft Parade*, and the growing distance from his poetry, literature, and films he cared about, contributed to his poor attitude. The same could be said of himself, the band, and the pack of lies his generation had been sold about life and liberty in the land of the free. But there was still one place to go: Composing "in a blues vein... Long, rambling, basic, and primitive," the blues would ease his troubled mind and provide a hiding place from the Miami debacle, and his thoughts of women, from India to Indio. Though Densmore had yet to become a fan of the 12-bar, 4/4 time of the form ("Basically he likes jazz," was how Jim summed up his bandmate's position) and Krieger's interests remained an international smorgasbord of riffs, the blues weren't exactly a hard sell either: The band knew better than to resist their singer who proved to be most capable when he was pursuing the things he wanted. What Jim wanted, what he needed, was to get back to basics.

"I think in this country we keep returning to blues and country because they're our two indigenous musical forms," said Morrison in the 1969 *Rolling Stone* interview. Like other prime rock artists of his generation, Morrison recognized rock's past and future lived in the blues; the back-to-roots approach was also the current trend in rock 'n' roll (the Beatles "Get Back" sessions would become *Let It Be*, and the Stones were cutting songs by Robert Wilkins and Robert Johnson for *Beggar's Banquet* and *Let It Bleed*). The blues, a "sustained poetic attack on the superstructure of an exploitative society,"[13] according to author Paul Garon, was the perfect sound for the breakdown that was 1969.

At a time when Morrison was further accessing his own pain regarding the tyranny of an American identity, his additional performance rituals provided a theatrical component to his expression of discontent, while his inhabitance of a Dionysian guise better transmitted that power to the people. Alongside Jimi Hendrix and Janis Joplin, few Americans were as convincing or as charismatic as Morrison, leading the charge for total freedom.

And then there was Jimbo, determined to undermine the cause at every turn.

Whatever method Morrison was using to try to quit drinking wasn't working. Anxious and in anticipation of his trial still many months away, at the end of the year, another public drunk scene made the press: Jim and a friend were accused of abusing a stewardess on a short flight from LA to Phoenix. No amount of outlaw poetry and political theater, experimental French existential film, Dionysian spectacle, psychological technique of dominance and control or shamanism – all things Morrison used to control his interior landscape – could control the effects of drugs and alcohol on his physical self. Between the bad reviews, performance difficulties, and increased frustration within the band surrounding Jim's public outbursts, private meltdowns, and general unreliability, the Doors had reached the end of their second act. It was going to take drastic measures, perhaps a miracle, to return from the brink and bounce back. Taking stock following two years of steady recording, the back-to-back release of four albums, and the heavy roadwork with Jim's problems on board, as much as the other Doors loved the shapes, sizes, and studio experimentation of jazz, the blues were the medicine for a sick and tired band at their crossroads as the decade closed.

CHAPTER 7

Back to Basics: 1969-1970

"I just remember that some of the best musical trips we took were in clubs,"[1] said Morrison. Back when they were still a local band from Venice, audiences responded when the Doors let the black snake moan and threw down the classics, from "King Bee" to "Little Red Rooster." Hoping to capture some of the old blues magic that launched them, in November of 1969, the band rolled into the studio and began their sessions at Elektra Sound Recorders in Hollywood by shaking loose some of the old numbers: They dusted off their rendition of "Money," and tried out new jams like "Rock is Dead," an attempt to traverse the history of blues, rock, surf, and Latin styles all in one song.

The blues was almighty and all that was holy and good about rock 'n' roll; it also provided a focus for Jim in the studio while he wrote the majority of the songs for the band's fifth album, *Morrison Hotel*. There is the deep funk, soul, and rich New Orleans roll to "Peace Frog," (with its riff on Morrison's poem, "Dawn's Highway") and "Road House Blues," ragged but tough, was inspired by

Morrison's Topanga nights with Canned Heat: *The future's uncertain and the end is always near.*

Accompanied by the Lovin' Spoonful's John Sebastian on harmonica (credited as G. Puglese), hotshot guitarist Lonnie Mack (who mostly played bass), and bassist Ray Neapolitan, the sessions were once again overseen by a now increasingly fatigued and frustrated Paul Rothchild, alongside his easier-going engineer, Bruce Botnick. Falling readily into the mix, "Indian Summer," a leftover take from the band's very first session, was reborn. Recounting his initial parting from Mary Werbelow when he made his journey from St. Petersburg to Tallahassee, "Indian Summer" was among Morrison's first summer of '65 songs; four years later, there was no mistaking its subject. With Mary truly gone and unreachable in India, "Indian Summer" had become an invocation, with the added dimension of the Far East confluence (the song would become a standout favorite among Doors fans on the Asian subcontinent). Yet another held over song, "Waiting for the Sun," spoke of a yearning to connect with a distant lover.

"I think my favorite is *Morrison Hotel*," said Jim of the record. "Just in the respect that we didn't use any other musicians, except a bass player."[2] Taking its title from a squalid SRO building on Skid Row, the album cover was shot on location in LA on the corner of Pico and Hope Streets, where the Morrison Hotel structure remains.

"It was pretty weird when we went to the Morrison Hotel in downtown LA to photograph their album cover and the guy behind the desk wouldn't let us take any pictures," remembered photographer Henry Diltz. "As we walked outside, I noticed through the window that the guy left the desk and got in the elevator. I said, 'Quick! Run in there and get behind the window!' I shot one roll of film and we were out of there."[3]

With a gritty and realist exterior to match the music's lowdown aural energy, the *Morrison Hotel* package was a major contributor to a trend toward the natural in rock 'n' roll style and album covers in the '70s. The Doors' homegrown art even evolved in an initially organic way: Manzarek scouted the location, and the band was already comfortable with Diltz, known to them from earlier Venice Beach days. As they paused during the shoot, to quench their thirst at The Hard Rock Café, a workingman's dive bar on Fifth and Wall Streets in the heart of Skid Row, Diltz captured the back cover, and the work was done. (The original Hard Rock Café no longer stands, though an unrelated chain of restaurants and hotels all over the world became monuments to side one of *Morrison Hotel*).

Skid Row, Los Angeles

The area designated as Central City East (bordered by Third and Seventh Streets from the north and south, and Alameda and Main Streets from the east and west, the center of downtown Los Angeles) is also known as Skid Row. Established in the late 19th Century as a district housing transient workers and resident hotels, today it is known for containing the largest so-called stable population of homeless people in the US. Estimated at about 4,000 homeless persons living on the street there, there's an overall estimated 200,000 individuals in

LA County who are living homeless. In June 2012, the Health Department declared the neighborhood a hazard and began a cleanup program following the discovery of rats' nests, hypodermic needles, and human feces on the streets there.

The City of Los Angeles has centralized its health, social welfare, and rescue missions on Skid Row, ostensibly to better serve its hard-pressed residents, though it has long been rumored and indeed confirmed that law enforcement and city services from other jurisdictions send their mentally ill and indigent population to the area for its concentration of support services. A relatively humane attitude prevails in treating the mentally and physically disabled, addicted, and down-and-out population there, precisely because it is widely acknowledged that the city has not provided enough beds for people in need; sleeping on the street has been tolerated and will be until a time more shelters can be provided, though there are periodic crackdowns and sweeps of people and their belongings by LAPD.

Skid Row is an extremely dysfunctional and unfortunate reality of Los Angeles life and of life in the United States of America, where thousands of people have no idea when they will taste their next meal or rest their heads safely for the night. Ironically, the billion-dollar industry that is Hollywood and its studios rests within a few miles from Skid Row: The contrasting conditions between the two worlds are not easily ignored by anyone who has eyes, ears, or a heart. KPCC radio host Patt Morrison has made coverage of the area her priority, as has *Los Angeles Times* reporter Steve Lopez whose columns about the area were turned into the feature film, *The Soloist*. Starring Robert Downey Jr. and Jamie Foxx, the dramatized story lines up with hard reports of living with mental illness on the streets that generations after generations of Angelenos call home.[4]

It is the author's hope that erecting facilities to house the citizenry of the City of Angels becomes a greater priority in years to come. Let Jim Morrison's relationship to Los Angeles remain a reminder and an appeal to those in a position to help its souls on Skid Row.

"Ship of Fools," a parable of a passenger ship at sea without a captain, inspired by Morrison's favorite Hieronymus Bosch painting, could have easily have been written in the 21st Century:

The human race was dying out
no one left to scream and shout
people walking on the moon
smog gon' get you pretty soon

"Ship of Fools" was the first in a wave of songs with the same title (the Grateful Dead song, written by Jerry Garcia and his writing partner, poet Robert Hunter, was included on their 1974 album, *From The Mars Hotel*, named for a residential hotel on downtown San Francisco's Fourth Street; their song also rhymes "wild" with "child").

Conjuring "what the men don't know, the little girls understand" from Willie Dixon's "Back Door Man," Morrison's own road-weary self ends the album with the apocalyptic blues, "Maggie M'gill."

Well I'm an old blues man,
and I think that you understand
I've been singing the blues
ever since the world began

An intensely real performance, it captures Morrison at the beginning of the end.

Illegitimate son of a rock'n'roll star
illegitimate son of a rock'n'roll star
mom met dad in the back of a rock'n'roll car

"One of the most convincing, raunchy vocals Jim Morrison has ever recorded," wrote rock critic Lester Bangs of "Roadhouse Blues" in his *Rolling Stone* album review upon the release of *Morrison Hotel* in February 1970. Notorious for his own use of intoxicants and for his sharp attacks, Bangs praised the album, and noted its angry, brooding tones. Other reviews were also generally positive, an indication the new year and *Morrison*

Hotel could mark a new beginning and positive cycle of creativity for the Doors, despite the predictable season of discontent that lay ahead.

While the trial date in Miami loomed, the Doors traveled to New York for the beginning of the *Roadhouse Blues* tour at Felt Forum. Documenting the performances, with an eye on compiling a summer live release, Morrison revealed to *Rolling Stone*, his vision for a Doors concert album featuring rock 'n' roll classics and the blues. Explaining had they tried that kind of repertoire any sooner than 1970, "I think it would've looked like we'd run out of things to say," he said. But five albums in, the Doors had achieved stature to record whatever combination of songs they saw fit; not all were in agreement with this fact. Elektra was neutral, calling *Absolutely Live* an "organic documentary." Gloria Tanjak of *Rolling Stone* claimed, "What's theater on the stage is garbage on the turntable." And Paul Rothchild, still not confident of the band's capabilities, claimed there were over 2,000 edits of the performances on the "live" album. On the positive side, Morrison finally got to commit a performance of "The Celebration of the Lizard" to tape, filling one whole side of the double record set. Fragments of text from "Not to Touch the Earth," and "Go Insane" (the song that so infuriated the record executive who refused to sign them in 1965), comprise a section of the piece, an ode to non-violent revolution inspired by Percy Bysshe Shelley's *The Masque of Anarchy*.

One morning he awoke in a green hotel
With a strange creature groaning beside him
Sweat oozed from its shining skin

During the Door's New York run, Patricia Kennealy interviewed Jim for *Jazz and Pop* magazine and the pair began their affair. Morrison and Kennealy formed a bond rooted in their shared pursuit of spiritual and intellectual concerns. She is among the old friends who claim that rarely, if ever, did she see Morrison's notorious dark side. In June of 1970, their liaison culminated in a pagan ritual marriage ceremony known as handfasting. While the other Doors claim never to have met her (Robby Krieger has referred to her as "that witch"), Kennealy took the name Morrison, and maintains she and Jim were married, though by her own admission, he likely didn't take their vows seriously. In the years since their acquaintance, Kennealy became known for her own writing beyond rock, as well as for the intense period of time she spent with Morrison.

The pair hung out with Elektra's Jac Holzman and music writer Ellen Sander. Likening his role as a rock star to the troubadours of France, Morrison was finding a piece of contentment within the circle of rock, the culture of his age. "I'm pleased to be alive at this time," he said. "It seems romantic to me… I think we're going to look very good to future people, because so many changes are taking place and we're really handling it with flair."[5] His generation's sounds, its fashions, and its women excited him. He had an appreciation of the freedoms the youth culture had won and he understood the significance of cultural and social shifts, their historical precedents and contexts. But as sure as he was wresting some enjoyment from life, there would be haters: A reporter for *The Village Voice* saw Morrison on the New York scene and seized on his appearance, describing him as "chubby" and with a "hairline receding." A more thoughtful talk in the alternative weekly focused on his taste in contemporary music.

"I like the old blues singers about the best," Morrison told Howard Smith. "Stravinsky, I like him. I like the early rock 'n' roll people, the classic dudes, and some of the modern English groups, I like. Some of our local talent is also very good. But there're so many rock musicians, it'd be impossible to single out one or two or three. I think we have some excellent music happening. When you think about the excellent music that's been written in the last ten years, it boggles the mind." As for Dylan, "I think he just keeps getting better and better."[6]

Just as his generation had taken the reigns of rock and turned it into a cultural expression for their time, the next generation was standing in line, readying themselves to take over. Morrison was happy to voice his future of music theories to anyone who'd listen to those too. He knew the end of the '60s marked another little death on the road to rock 'n' roll, that the end of the modern era at the gateway to post-modernism would allow for a reinvention of rock 'n' roll based largely on its roots of rebellion. Morrison even went as far as to suggest what the uprising would be, and what it might look like: "So maybe after the Vietnam war is over... there will again be a life force that needs to express itself, to assert itself."[7] It was as if Morrison could see and hear the rebel music forces of reggae, punk rock, and hip hop, fermenting on the horizon.

Rock on Trial

There is perhaps no better illustration of the undoing of Jim Morrison than the situations he confronted from spring of 1969 until the fall 1970 trial in Miami. Just a small run-in with the law could derail even the most well-balanced of personalities, but for an already precariously loaded artist/performer/provocateur/hard-drinker/blues singer like Morrison, it was like being put to the test: the year of stops and starts, cancelled engagements, and the media spotlight on the alleged obscenity charges were breaking him down.

"It's like a political football, you know," he told the *Village Voice*. "They'll let us sign up for a concert and then about two days before we show up, the mayor or the sheriff or somebody, whoever wants to get his name in the paper will try and cancel the show and get everyone all outraged," he explained. "People, parents who wouldn't even know who we were, all of a sudden they hear that 'Sheriff Peabody says, they shouldn't be allowed to perform' – like that."[8]

His perception and illustration of the broken pact between the artist and audience, artist and country, and artist and culture, was a heavy weight for any American poet to carry. To be painted by the media as the counterculture's representative of all that was threatening and unsavory was certainly discomfiting, but Morrison was no fool: He knew precisely what was at stake leading up to the show trial in Miami.

"What we're testing down there is the issue of artistic freedom of expression. It's a significant issue and the trial is very interesting,"[9] he said.

"You seem confident," noted one reporter.

"Hopefully it'll be over in time for me to do a European tour," said Morrison.

It was wishful thinking. As a calendar year of cancelled tour dates carried over into August, September, and October, the timetable for Morrison's troubles overlapped with the ramping up of the government's well-documented efforts to shut down the counterculture and disempower it. The largely covert counter-intelligence operation (COINTELPRO) was discovered years later to be on the order of J. Edgar Hoover's FBI. Morrison's file is nearly 100 pages; though he was not perceived to be a threat as great as organized political action and activism groups, he was not alone among rockers of his stature in being pursued by the authorities who compiled papers and kept under surveillance people perceived to be charismatic and influential youth leaders.

As the obscenity trial kicked off in Dade County, it became even clearer that Morrison had become a pawn in the game of municipal political chess. With the judge, attorney, and police chief serving out "acting status" terms, their positions were all in a state of flux, and Morrison became a victim of them jockeying for position in his politically corrupt home state. There were no accommodations for the band's scheduling considerations, no allowance for the career they were attempting to sustain, nor any understanding that Morrison was an artist with something to say, making a contribution to society. The trial did nothing to serve the well being of the community, nor did it do anything positive for the Doors, increasing as it did their renown for cancellations and unreliability.

In Miami, Morrison was convicted and given six months hard labor, and a fine. He planned to appeal, while the insistence with which the law pursued him was unrelenting. Called off dates continued to haunt the band – from Mexico City and across the states – and Morrison's, reputation, now always in question, took a further hit as his stability was continuously in doubt or challenged. On the nights he drank, he'd have to take responsibility for that, though even under duress he maintained that he never did what they said he did in Miami.

"I told you, we're the band you love to hate," he told Howard Smith. "I could write an American folk song, something that would appeal to everyone, and everyone would say gee what a great guy." Instead, he thought about writing and directing a film, and prepared to return to Elektra Recorders for another blues-based album, but Miami had taken a toll on him.

"He was definitely a little rough. The whole trial thing was hanging over his head and all that. He wasn't feeling that well health-wise. I remember him coughing and spitting up blood probably from smoking too many cigarettes...." remembered Robby Krieger. It is believed that Morrison may've had asthma that was untreated, and there is no doubt alcoholism contributed to his ill health.

The pursuit of Morrison around the Miami incident, like the unfounded investigations of Jimi Hendrix, Janis Joplin, the MC5, John Lennon, and countless poets and activists of the '60s generation, proved to be an abuse of power and waste of tax dollars. As the trial rolled, the official government documents pertaining to Morrison did make one thing crystal clear: A collation of his arrest records, eleven in all, beginning in 1963 and ending in 1969 with the in-flight incident with the stewardess, had one word that appeared repeatedly: drunk. It's not a condition usually associated with threatening the national security, but it's a salient point and final detail in the portrait of the artist as an alcoholic.

Mojo on the Rise

He was the Lizard King; he could do anything. Or could he? "What I was trying to say in that… that was years ago, and even then I meant it ironically," explained Jim in 1970. "That whole thing was done half tongue-in-cheek. I just thought everyone knew I meant it ironically but apparently they thought I meant it." Back-pedaling on his self-created myth, Morrison's mix-ups and muddying of his artistic vision while piling on personae were, among other things, ways to cope with his discomfort as a public figure and rock star. He entered a new phase of his blues.

In the summer of 1970, the Doors were joined onstage in Vancouver by bluesmen Albert King who sat in for "Little Red Rooster," 'Money," "Rock Me," and "Who Do You Love." Having forged a bond early on with the original country bluesman and the first generation of R&B shouters and rock 'n' rollers of Chicago, Morrison's new character was utterly masculine, hard drinking, and hard loving. Using time-honored catch phrases and potent imagery, he was getting closer to a more naturalistic Jim. Shedding the skin of the Lizard King was in itself a demonstration of shamanistic power, and hoodoo magic, a portent of other realms and possibilities. It was also an attempt to wash the slate clean of the complications of the performing arts and the aesthetics that enveloped him. Staking his claim, becoming who he wanted to be, this penultimate guise corresponded with a bigger Jim, more hirsute, rugged, and bedraggled. Waving goodbye to the black mamba and all that encumbered him, the time had come for the anagrammatic Mr. Mojo Risin'.

CHAPTER 8

LA Women: 1970-1971

In the early 1970s, Elektra became less Jac Holzman's classical/folk/international musical vision and more of a standard enterprise when Kinney National, soon to be rechristened Warner Communications, acquired the label. Morrison pondered the merger, among other concerns, during an interview on the scene with John Tobler of rock magazine *Zig Zag* at the Isle of Wight Festival in August of 1970 – a make-up date following the chaotic year of the trial.

"Now that they've become part of a corporation, it'll be interesting to see if the company gets better or if they kinda get assimilated," he said. "Hopefully it might give them a chance not to worry about competing in the popular field and do the thing they do best… classical, experimental things, folk things. Give a chance to the people that haven't been given a chance to get commercially successful in their own time. Maybe it'll give them a chance to get back to that. I think with us, it was really a freak thing, they never repeated that," said Morrison of his band's success.

"They had Love, and someone associated with them, brought them to see us," said Morrison. "Love was the popular underground group at the time. We figured, if they went on Elektra, it must be a good label. It's too bad about Love... they weren't willing to travel and to go through all the games and numbers that you have to do to get it out to a large number of people. If they had done that, I think they could've been as big as anyone. And someday they will," asserted Morrison. From their outpost at the London Fog, "The Doors from Venice," had once dreamed of being as popular as Love; by 1970, they'd outstretched that band's success by a million miles and Love, as they were known, had fallen apart. Arthur Lee and his new band continued to record and release records; in 1970 he was working on a track with Jimi Hendrix called "The Everlasting First," which opened Love's sixth album, *False Start*. Hendrix was also famously at the Isle of Wight Concert that year: he played for the last time on the evening of the five-day festival's final night. The Doors had played the previous night.

Not best seen in daylight, "I don't think our particular music style holds up very well in a huge outdoor event," said Morrison, perhaps in some way explaining away the fact the Doors had missed both the Monterey and Woodstock festivals (though they did appear at the Fantasy Fair and Magic Mountain Music Festival at Mount Tamalpais, Marin County, California, in 1967, quite possibly the first modern outdoor music festival). He told his interviewer he wasn't impressed with the film version of *Woodstock*: "Young parasites spoon-fed three or four days...they looked like victims and dupes of the culture." Given his limited experience of festival concerts, he wasn't shy about asserting his opinion of them. "Even if they aren't what they tend to be, some free celebration of a young culture, it's still better than nothing. And I'm sure some of the people take some myth back to the city with them." Refusing illumination, even after dark, the Doors' performances of "When the Music's Over" and "The End" at Isle of Wight, as seen in the film, *Message to Love*, portray a fairly relaxed Morrison in the festival setting.

In the same interview, Morrison opened up a bit about his family and upbringing – a far cry from where he started as a Door, proclaiming them dead – yet the comment is edged in innuendo. "So many schools. I traveled around a lot…a different school a year. Every year and a half I went to a different one," he said. "That's the best part of this business. You get to travel around a lot."[1]

That September, Al Wilson of Canned Heat died in Topanga Canyon of a barbiturate overdose. And not long after the Isle of Wight, on September 18, Jimi Hendrix died in London, the circumstances mysterious and controversial for decades, though in all likelihood, drug and alcohol poisoning contributed. Sixteen days later, Janis Joplin was found dead of a heroin overdose at the Landmark Motor Hotel in Los Angeles, discovered when she didn't show up to a recording session with Paul Rothchild at Sunset Sound. "Who's next" was the subconscious and sensationalist thread, a pervasive thought in rock circles.

As the year wound down and the Miami appeal ground on, for his 27th birthday on December 8, 1970, Jim went to Village Recorders at 1616 Butler Ave. in West Los Angeles to commit some of his poems – three hours worth – to tape. Perhaps it was an acknowledgment of sorts that life is short, and one must seize the time. A few days later, the Doors left town to fulfill final tour dates for the year, finishing their concert calendar with a creepy show in New Orleans which by all accounts was not a good night.

Overheated and inebriated, Jim couldn't finish the set; Mr. Mojo did not rise, and the poor performance was alternately attributed to the dripping hot weather, Louisiana lawlessness, the spirit of *laissez les bon temps rouler*, or a voodoo curse cast upon them. Deciding then and there that their performing days were through, the Doors returned home to commence recording their sixth album, though immediately there were problems with that too.

The vibe at the Elektra studio appeared to be lost and no longer serving them, and the band considered moving back to Sunset Sound, scene of their previous triumphs, before deciding the rehearsal room was the right spot for recording. Moving an eight-track recorder into their workshop on La Cienega – forsaking the extra eight tracks they'd experimented with on the *Soft Parade* – recording commenced.

The Producers

Paul Rothchild and Bruce Botnick are names forever associated with the Doors. Emerging from the Boston folk scene, Rothchild became producer at Elektra beginning in 1963. In 1964 he discovered Paul Butterfield and in 1966, he recorded the Butterfield Blues Band's

groundbreaking *East-West* album, which introduced the extended jam and a bit of jazz to rock. Relocating to LA, ensconced in the Laurel Canyon scene, he worked with all the big names from Crosby, Stills and Nash, to Joni Mitchell and Neil Young; he also oversaw production of the soundtrack to the film, *The Doors*. Rothchild died of lung cancer in 1995.

In addition to assisting Rothchild on the first five Doors albums and producing *LA Woman* with the Doors, Bruce Botnick engineered Love's albums and co-produced with Arthur Lee *Forever Changes* (its orchestrated West Coast psychedelic rock became another watershed in Elektra's catalog and over time could claim status as an album of influence). Following his successes with Jim Morrison and Arthur Lee, at the end of the '70s, Botnick enjoyed success as a producer of hitmaker Eddie Money then moved into film soundtrack recording and mixing.

Within ten days (an extremely short time by '70s recording standards), *LA Woman* was made – without producer Paul Rothchild. Still reeling from the loss of Janis Joplin with whom he was working at the time of her death, Rothchild was also still not convinced the Doors were up to the task of writing and recording a record without extreme studio intervention. But perhaps more to the point, he found it increasingly intolerable to be around Morrison. "Two out of three times, Jim would either not want to work or go into the studio drunk,"[2] as he recalled it. On the other side of the argument, after five albums in a two and a half year period together, the Doors had gained the experience and artistic credibility to dictate the direction of their own recording: Robby Krieger had in turn tired of Rothchild, and the producer's orientation toward detail and perfection. Dubbing him the "king of slow," Rothchild's demands to recut songs, take after take after take, had worn down the band, and critics inside and outside their orbit cited the overwrought tapes as sucking the life out of a once vital act. If a loose and more unkempt sound is what they were after, so be it.

"We were so far gone that it was like a weight was lifted when Paul left," said Kreiger. "Jim had been pretty uninvolved on some of the albums but he was right there with us on this and that's what made it so special."[3]

Pamela Courson was also out of the picture in the early recording window for *LA Woman* – at least temporarily. She was in Paris with Count Jean de Breuteuil, her on/off boyfriend, until Christmas. A playboy and drug dealer of some renown among the rock 'n' roll elite, the Count's international connections from France to Morocco kept him in large supply of drugs and largely out of trouble.

Upon Pam's return, in early 1971 Jim was generally hanging out at the apartment at 8214 W. Norton, another one of his landing pads away from the motel madness. Elektra Records publicist Diane Gardiner lived in the same complex; a lover of roots music, she and Jim were close, and he liked to thumb through her record collection, getting into her blues. Gardiner's apartment was a good hang, a place to hide and saturate himself in music and music people, like the day *Rolling Stone* reporter, Ben Fong-Torres, dropped by and got Jim to talk about whether the word on the street was true: Were the Doors making a blues album?

"That's what I was hoping this album would turn out to be…that's what we do best," said Morrison. "We're using Elvis' bass player," he said, referring to Jerry Scheff. "For the first time, we're recording it in our office, where we rehearse. We're using the same engineer, that we use on our other records, Bruce Botnick, but we're not using Paul. It was kinda mutual. I guess we figured we'll just take different roads." Botnick was simpatico with what the Doors were trying to do. "He's a young guy, very easy to work with,"[4] said Morrison.

The band thought they had a hit single on their hands with the psychedelic soul jam "The Changeling," but Elektra's Jac Holzman disagreed and it was decided the more mainstreamed pop cut, "Love Her Madly," would be released as the single. The album largely lives up to Morrison's idea of "original blues if there is such a thing," riffing on the music's shapes and themes.

"Car Hiss By My Window," is the Doors' homage to popular electric bluesman, Jimmy Reed. "I started playing in E and this song just happened," said Krieger. "She Smells So Nice," recorded at the sessions but left unreleased for 40 years, slides into "Rock Me," the old blues jam, wherein Jim also riffs on Mr. Mojo Risin'; the song had been in the repertoire for the life of the band.

"The Wasp (Texas Radio and the Big Beat)" follows an unpredictable pattern. "A lot of these songs seem easy to play but they're not,"[5] explained Kreiger. The guitarist says the Doors owed their unorthodox melodies and practices to inexperience, citing "extra bars and inconsistent turnarounds." A demo of "Hyacinth House" was recorded on a four- track portable machine at Kreiger's house where hyacinths were a feature of the garden. The lyrics were mundane references to things Morrison saw and overheard on the grounds there ("I see the bathroom's clear now"); the lion in the verse was Kreiger's pet bobcat.

"Been Down So Long," was recorded live, "with Marc [Benno] playing the rhythm, so I could just play the leads, fills, and slide," explained Kreiger years later. The phrase "been down so long" was hardly unique by 1971 and Morrison certainly didn't coin it, though in blues tradition he had appropriated it. The 1967 novel, *Been Down So Long It Looks Like Up to Me* by folk musician Richard Fariña was known well in counter-culture circles. Fariña would've likely taken the phrase "Been down so long it looks like up to me" from the Furry Lewis song, "Turn Your Money Green." Ishman Bracey had *been down so long, down don't worry me* in "Trouble-Hearted Blues," as was Billie Holiday who famously sang the same line in "Stormy Blues." An aphorism used to cope with poverty, grief, and longing, in the early '60s J.B. Lenoir performed an entirely different slow blues, "Been Down So Long." There were plenty of other variations on the phrase, but when Morrison took it on, blues purists went nuts – it sounded like a parody. Perhaps they could not hear in his delivery that Jim was down, compromised, and perilously close to never getting up again.

"Riders on the Storm" evolved out of a jam on the cowboy legend, "Ghost Riders in the Sky." The much-covered country song with the "yippie-ti-ay" chorus is less benign than it sounds: It tells the story of cattlemen who are consigned to an interminable rough ride in hell, sent to pay for their sins on earth against man and nature. "Riders on the Storm" suggests that the spirits of heaven and hell are present in the here and now. Rooted in Americana and real-time happenings, all of the songs on *LA Woman* were strangely unique and forward pushing – thoroughly modern but eerily familiar.

"I was saying rock was dead years ago… Every five or ten years, everyone comes together and swarms then they break apart and come back," Morrison said in 1971. "When you think about rock it's a definite 4/4, physical body movement trip. It's not mind music, I don't think. For example, if you couldn't understand the words, there'd still be everything there to react to."

Speaking to questions of his own shape shifting and changing physicality, he told *Village Voice* reporter Howard Smith he weighed an unlikely 150 pounds. "You know, that's something that really bothers me… what's wrong with fat… It's terrible to be thin and wispy because you could get knocked over by a strong wind or something, you know? Fat is beautiful." The statuesque Dionysus, the teenage idol, of bare chest and ringlets, had officially sought retirement. "I must admit there were occasions where having a reputation like that did help me out in some tight situations," says Jim. "Plus I got to meet a lot of groovy ladies who probably would've otherwise not've noticed me, so in that respect it was all to the good." Laying it on thick, Morrison delivered a performance of a lifetime in one of his rare surviving audio interviews of this period. Incorporating psychological manipulation, and shock principles from the Living Theater and the Theater of Cruelty, Morrison plays it California rocker cool, yet at the same time he is worldly aware, surreal, poetic, cinematic, philosophic, and absurd. Mr. Mojo had given rise and made way for the real Jim Morrison to come out to play: His timeless intellect, keen self-awareness, and fine-tuned sense humor were all miraculously, still perfectly intact.

CHAPTER 9

Au Revoir LA

"That's actually the last time Jim Morrison was in a recording studio, the last time he ever sang with the Doors on planet earth. That haunted little whisper voice on "Riders on the Storm,"[1] remembered Ray Manzarek. "I'm going to Paris, he said." Morrison took his films, *HWY* and *Feast of Friends*, his poetry manuscripts, his notebooks, a few paperbacks, and some clothes and moved to 17 Rue Beautreillis in the fourth arrondissement. The apartment belonged to a friend of Pam's who came and went from it on business. The couple also occupied L'Hôtel, on the rue des Beaux-Arts, known to be the place where Oscar Wilde died.

Mazarek thought Paris was a great idea. "The city of light, the city of artists… Get away from all this LA stuff, this whole rock and roll thing. Become a poet again. Become the guy I knew back in Venice, the guy that I knew back in film school at UCLA: the writer, the artist, the good guy, the good human being, the funny human being, the intelligent, sensitive, energized young man, that I knew back in Venice."

Going about his life in Paris, Morrison was making time to devote to writing. He reportedly eased up on drinking, but he was soon as messed up as Pam, who by that time had developed a serious heroin habit. Jim's general health had reportedly begun deteriorating with signs of spitting up blood and a prescription from a doctor suggesting a vacation in a warm climate. The pair set off for a pleasant trip to Spain and Marrakech, returning again to Paris.

"There are only two choices you can make: Each of us had made it,"[2] Morrison said to Alain Ronay, his friend from film school, also living in Paris at the time. "You and I are on the side of life, she is on the side of death," Jim told him. "Neither you nor I can do anything about it. Don't worry about her." Ambling around Paris, walking and talking, Morrison asked Ronay if he would mind a stop at the local cemetery, Père Lachaise. Ronay reports Morrison as so taken by its location, the scenery, and serene vibe, that he told his friend someday, like Honoré de Balzac and Oscar Wilde, he hoped to be buried there, among the *hommes de lettres*.

Encouraged by Michael McClure, Morrison had self-published *The Lords: Notes on Vision* and *The New Creatures*. Concerning established societal order, the voice in his writings kicked against convention and took in ideas on philosophy, performance, and film.

All games contain the idea of death

Allusions to lone gunmen, assassins, vagrants, the military brat, wandering minstrel, international vagabond, sex symbol, troubadour, the romantic with a shaman's blues, and the outsider in his own band were all directly poems about "the powerlessness that people have in the face of reality. They have no real control over events or their own lives. Something is controlling them. The closest they get is the television set."[3]

Something more powerful than self controlled Morrison too: Drinking whiskey, roaming, he'd become alternately engaging and withdrawn, a Jekyll and Hyde remixed. Legend has long had it he booked studio time with a pair of street musicians (though more likely he used the time to simply transfer the tapes he brought to Paris – an impromptu jam of "Orange County Suite," with its essence of Pam).

Well I used to know someone fair
She had orange ribbons in her hair
She was such a trip, she was hardly there
But I loved her just the same

In April, *LA Woman* was released, and the reception to it at home and abroad was extraordinarily positive, a "new, more mature musical direction." Despite the Doors' trials and legal matters in Miami still pending, and their growing reputation as erratic performers, "Love Her Madly" was a hit, as Holzman and Elektra predicted it would be. It was against this celebratory backdrop of a rebirth that John Densmore began to fear Jim might return from Paris: the dreaded phone call came.

"He can't come back I thought," remembered Densmore of his talk with Jim. "He would just want to play the blues, the slow, soulful monotonous blues, which is great for a singer like him but boring for a drummer like me,"[4] he wrote in *Riders on the Storm*. Years later Robby Krieger said he did in fact perceive a future in which the Doors went deeper into their blues. "I really feel that if you're a real band, jamming can be the best way to write songs. You discover things and latch onto great riffs and interlocking parts and we were doing that more and more with Jim becoming more involved in these sessions. I truly believe... we would've continued in that direction."

Ray Manzarek agreed. "The Doors were a blues band with literary aspirations."

Densmore was still not buying it: "If he reappeared, I saw us spending the rest of our lives in dumpy clubs and grumpy recording sessions. We're not going down to the Golden Bear-kind-of-dives with the old blues man. No way Jose."[5]

A Death in Paris

"On July 3, 1971, Jim Morrison died in Paris under what can only be called mysterious circumstances,"[6] said Manzarek. Pamela Courson was with him, but as told to police and assorted friends, her version of the story was reportedly different every time she recounted it. "We don't know what happened to Jim in Paris, and I don't think we're ever going to know what happened to Jim in Paris," was Manzarek's take on it. Over 40 years later, the night remains shrouded in mystery.

The following is a crude approximation of the events leading up to Morrison's passing. Maybe he and Pam went to the Rock 'n' Roll Circus (formerly known as the Whisky A-Go Go); maybe they'd gone to the movies, and for Chinese food, and gone back to the apartment to watch home movies of their recent travels, drink some whisky, and snort some heroin. Becoming increasingly drowsy, enraged and blotto, Jim had a meltdown (neighbors report as much), then one of the pair drew a bath, and he locked the door behind him.

According to Alain Ronay who received the call early Saturday morning at filmmaker Agnès Varda's home, Courson reported Morrison had stopped breathing. Ronay and Varda set out for the apartment and the pair tended to Courson the best they could, serving as French-speaking liaisons with authorities. But it is widely suspected among those in the know that Jean De Breteuil had been Pam's first call. The Count had already been to the apartment, removing from it any trace of drugs or his connection to them. That night, De Breteuil set off for Morocco with singer Marianne Faithfull.

It was determined that a combination of drugs, alcohol, respiratory problems, heart failure, natural causes, heroin overdose, or all of the above landed Morrison in the bathtub, vomiting blood and the previous evening's Chinese dinner. The medical examiner estimated his age as 57, but Jim was only in the middle of his 27th year. Removed from the bath and laid on the bed, he lay there for the next few days, Pam sleeping beside him. In death, as in life, circumstances surrounding the identification of Morrison's body and his burial were chaotic; his unreliable partner and her part-time drug supplier boyfriend didn't help matters. Passing on the eve of the Fourth of July weekend in the United States, and without the benefit of instant communication, the rest of the group was not officially notified until after the holiday. The burial, at Père Lachaise on July 7, 1971, was attended by a handful of friends.

Père Lachaise Cemetery and Venice Poets Monument

Cemetière du Père Lachaise in the 20th arrondissement of Paris, is a public and non-denominational burial ground. Served by the metro lines 2 & 3, it is named for the Jesuit confessor to King Louis XIV. Among fellow artists, Morrison would likely appreciate being buried beside are: Paul Éluard, Max Ernst, Molière, Yves Montand, Honoré de Balzac, Édith Piaf, Frédéric Chopin, Colette, Marcel Proust, Irish writer Oscar Wilde, and fellow Americans, Isadora Duncan, Gertrude Stein, and Alice B. Toklas. Nonstop flights on Air France, Delta, and Air Tahiti Nui depart from LAX to Paris' Charles DeGaulle and Orly Airports daily. Tours of Père Lachaise may be arranged, though it is easy enough to locate Morrison's grave: In the 89th division, not far from Oscar Wilde, it is marked with a plaque, installed in later years by the Morrison family. *True to Himself* is how the inscription translates from the ancient Greek phrase, *KATA TON ΔAIMONA EAYTOY.*

Today, Venice is a touchstone for art and culture on the Westside of Los Angeles. The Venetian columns are still visible on Windward Avenue, though most of old Venice has vanished, surviving in bits and pieces, peeking between million dollar McMansions perched on its walk streets and canals. The beach and boardwalk, with its collection of merchants, locals, and tourists is frequently featured in Hollywood movies, and an easygoing beach style is a way of life for the people who call the place home. Longtime residents co-mingle with Hollywood's top players, drug dealers, and runaways. In the midst of a sea of humanity, an inordinate number of pit bull terriers and a mish-mosh of architecture, stands the Venice Poet's Monument to the left of the Windward entrance to the beach. Pieces of poems by Philomene Long and latter-day Venetians, Exene Cervenka and Viggo Mortensen, are carved into the stone as is a portion of Morrison's "The Soft Parade." Not far from the beach at Beyond Baroque, the Venice institution most devoted to the preservation of poetry in the area, a full schedule of literary events takes place most every night of the week. Providing a stage for visiting poets, the bookstore keeps in stock an extensive selection of small press poetry and chapbooks. Also near the monument, on the Venice boardwalk, is Sidewalk Books: One of the Westside's last standing independent bookstores, it carries a selection of alternative titles and local history books.

Venice also hosts a concentration of murals by local street artists (a guide may be available at Beyond Baroque). The Morrison mural by Rip Cronk (1811 Speedway) is perhaps one of the most recognized images in the area and another way to pay homage. To date, neither Los Angeles nor

Santa Monica has erected a permanent monument, marker, or installation specifically remembering Jim Morrison. Perhaps the best way to remember him is to ride the highway west and notice the tingle in the air: On any given moonlight drive, from downtown's Skid Row and West Hollywood's nightclubs to Topanga's bungalows and Venice Beach's bars and coffeehouses, the palpable spirit of Jim Morrison – awake and alive – envelopes Los Angeles.

CHAPTER 10

Since Then

"I really admire poets who can get up with or without a microphone in front of a group of people and start reciting their poetry," Jim Morrison once said. Though it wasn't until seven years after his death that his recorded poems would be set to music, in his lifetime, Morrison had set a tone and a theatrical arc for dramatic storytelling that would touch rock and rap performance for decades to come. As early as 1969, Morrison had what turned out to be a fairly clear picture of music's future.

"It might rely heavily on electronics, tapes. I can kind of envision one person with a lot of machines, tapes, and electronic set-ups, singing, or speaking and using machines,"[1] he said.

After death, Morrison hardly disappeared; it was more like he never went away. From his leather pants, billowing shirt, and writhing snake dance, to his hyper masculine voice, and his apocalyptic night trips, Morrison's style and mode of outrageous performance penetrated music culture in a massive way, its influence lingering well after the turn of the 21st Century.

Seeds of Influence

The Doors had already begun the recording of their seventh album, *Other Voices*, with Bruce Botnick, when they learned Jim had passed. Paying homage to his beloved blues, it is generally lighter in sound and scope than the other works in their recorded catalog. The single, "'Tightrope Ride' is one of them that was done for Jim, you know," said Krieger. "Wandering Musician" quoted directly from their bandmate's credo: "Don't tell me what to do." The Doors followed with *Full Circle* in 1972, before taking a long hiatus.

Just as Morrison had predicted at the end of the '60s, by the Vietnam war's end in 1975, a new kind of rock 'n' roll, spun from the urban fabric of New York City, was unfurling. Heading the list of so-called punk-poets were Patti Smith, Tom Verlaine, and Richard Hell. Progeny of the Beat Generation, the Blank Generation were inspired by the same style of poetic rage that inspired Jim Morrison in Venice Beach, from Arthur Rimbaud to Bob Dylan.

"In 1974, when I started working with the material that became *Horses*, a lot of our great voices had died. We'd lost Jimi Hendrix and Jim Morrison and Janis Joplin, and people like Robert Kennedy, Martin Luther King, and Malcolm X. There were so many losses so quickly. These people who were building a political and cultural voice. And it seemed that rock'n'roll was heading toward something different – something consumer-oriented and stadium-oriented. I felt new generations had to come and break everything apart. As Jim Morrison says, 'Break on through to the other side.' And I felt in the center, not quite the old generation, not quite the new generation. I felt like the human bridge, and I just thought you have to wake up. Wake them up,"[2] Smith told *The Guardian* in recent years.

Smith had seen Morrison and the Doors in 1967 and said she thought, "'I could do that.' I felt this strange kinship. You have to figure, I was just a girl from South Jersey working in a book store."[3] Closely aligned with the legacies of dead poets and rock stars, Smith carried on the poetic tradition that Morrison brought to rock. She has long been dubbed rock's poetic priestess, using the stage to conduct a Blakeian celebration, encouraging the gods and goddess within to participate in their own lives. She also uses her platform as a performing artist to take a political stand. Like Morrison, her incantations are often best delivered when she performs rather than reads from the pages of books.

"Jim Morrison was one of our great poets and unique performers. His body of work will always endure," she said.[4]

Morrison's outlaw variations on blues and its themes, as well as his extreme theatrics, also directly influenced rocker Iggy Pop, who came to prominence as a solo artist following his mid-'70s collaborations with David Bowie. Though nearly Morrison's contemporary – Iggy was signed with the Stooges to Elektra in 1969 – he too had witnessed one of the Doors' chaotic 1967 tour stops in Detroit, and was inspired to start a band. "Jim Morrison and Mick Jagger. That's who I wanted to be. In fact it was so obvious that they should've called me Mick Morrison," he said. Pop, born James Osterberg, shared Morrison's predisposition for substance abuse; he spent the '70s down and out on Sunset Strip, but the similarities pretty much stop there. Self-educated, rather than university taught, he left Michigan for Chicago where he got some firsthand experience checking out the blues masters at work. Cleaning up his life and health-style considerably, Iggy Pop survived well into the 21st Century, performing his always shirtless, sometimes pantless, Godfather-of-punk act; he is rarely if ever accused of conjuring Morrison or the Doors.

At the height of the punk rock movement, in 1978, the Doors rather unfashionably set Jim's poems to music on the album titled *An American Prayer*. Unfortunately, the Doors likely destroyed Morrison's original intent for his spoken word tracks: They used audio from films and studio banter to piece together the project (for example, audio was taken from film, *Hwy: An American Pastoral* – in essence, Morrison acting his words from a script, combined with trademark stage rage, with some serious attempts at reading). And had the Doors known then about the original cover art, a triptych – a beach, a city, a desert – commissioned by Jim by the then-young artist T.E. Breitenbach, they could've used it as their visual guide. Nevertheless, the resulting over-dramatic recitation set to confused fusion-rock jams sounds much better today than it did in punk's high water days: Ironically, *An American Prayer* continues to enjoy an ever-increasing cult following, precisely because of its very-'70s musical values and Morrison's over-the-top spoken presence.

In 1979, Francis Ford Coppola used "The End" in the opening as well as in the climactic horror scene to great and memorable effect in his epic Vietnam film *Apocalypse Now*; immediately upon release, the scene entered the American popular culture vernacular. In 1980, the first biography of Morrison, *No One Here Gets Out Alive*, was published, co-authored by *Rolling Stone* reporter Jerry Hopkins and former band staffer, Danny Sugerman. By 1981, Morrison hit the cover of *Rolling Stone* with the famous tag line, "He's hot, he's sexy and he's dead." The genie had escaped from the bottle and in great oral and written tradition, especially among a large teenaged network, the legend of Jim Morrison's life was being passed down. A new generation of worshippers came of age celebrating the Lizard King, the myth of Dionysus, and the proverbial societal outlaw who died young and stayed pretty. Morrison's artistry and the myriad of influence he'd compressed into his poetry and performance would largely be forgotten in the media feeding frenzy. The Doors reportedly sold more records that year than in any year during their life as a band.

'80s Resurgence and '90s Renaissance

In 1977, Exene Cervenka from Florida and John Doe of Baltimore, MD, met at a Venice poetry workshop. With bandmates Billy Zoom and DJ Bonebrake they formed X, the West's most enduring, poetic, and socially conscious punk rock band. In 1978, Cervenka was quoted in punk rock 'zine *Search and Destroy*: "I used to listen to Jim Morrison a lot, he had an influence on me, but it was a mixed-up crazy influence that I got rid of because it wasn't doing me any good. Songs I like by him are 'Soul Kitchen' and 'Lost Little Girl' and 'Love Me Two Times' because they're about real things." John Doe said, "I was attracted to the

Doors as a teen because of the dark imagery." "I liked the Doors' version of the ocean," said Exene, "Which was dark and scary. It wasn't the sunny beach that the other people liked – especially those who liked roller skating."[5]

In 1980, X recorded its watershed, futuristic dark punk rock album, Los Angeles, produced by Ray Manzarek whom they'd met hanging out at the Whisky. Featuring his organ sound (and the band's speedy version of "Soul Kitchen"), it's an eerie love letter to the LA underworld, updated for the doomed generation. Manzarek guided the young band through their process of recording take after take, with a firm but gentle hand. Los Angeles won every conceivable critics award for the year.

Half a world away, Englishman Ian Astbury fronted the heavy goth rock '80s band, the Cult. Adopting a theatrical/operatic delivery and Jim Morrison look, when his own band had run its course, he was asked to sit in as a vocalist with the living Doors. Pearl Jam's Eddie Vedder would go on to stand in as singer for the band at their 1993 induction into the Rock and Roll Hall of Fame. Ray Manzarek called Scott Weiland, of Stone Temple Pilots and Velvet Revolver, the only singer who could "fill Jim's leather pants," though that may have had more to do with Weiland's taste for drugs and alcohol and his leather-clad look, than for his art and influences. Nevertheless, it's true the bands of the Seattle grunge wave of the early '90s from Alice in Chains to the Screaming Trees and Soundgarden are heirs of Morrison's haunted vocals and the Doors super-masculine, hard rock side. The grunge scene's most famous son, Kurt Cobain, is often remembered in the same breath as Morrison for being a member of "The 27 Club" the hideously named curse that early-on claimed

Robert Johnson, Jimi Hendrix, Janis Joplin, the Rolling Stones' Brian Jones, and in later years a disproportionate number of hard-living rockers whose time came too young.

In 1991, Oliver Stone's biopic, *The Doors*, starring Val Kilmer as Morrison, was largely a hit with viewers, but a miss with the band and those who knew Jim. The film was especially loathed by Manzarek, unconvinced and dissatisfied by the depiction of an always drunken Jim. Too much focus on their psychedelic experience and less on the artistic elements of the Doors makes it difficult to watch, yet for over 20 years, the film provided an often mistaken main frame of reference for new generations of fans. More interesting is Tom DiCillo's 2009 documentary *When You're Strange* which incorporates high quality archival Doors footage, including the restored clips from *HWY*. Narrated by Johnny Depp, it tells the story of a band caught in the chaos of the '60s, as well as within the web of an alternately visionary and inebriated singer.

"Five to One" Revisited and "Takeover"

Morrison's dark, apocalyptic stories and his ideas on the future of music turned out to be quite prescient. The advent of sampling in the '80s would unlock another area for the Doors' music to sustain its presence in the culture, again, as if Jim had predicted it. Further elucidating his projection of lone musicians working with tapes and electronic equipment, he foretold 21st Century DJ and club culture and the tech explosion in music. "Whoever it is though, I'd like him to be really popular, to play at large concerts, not just be on records – at Carnegie Hall, to play at dances. By dances, I mean it wouldn't be a sitting-down-and-listening-to type show. With milling around, you know?"

An iconic risk-taker, remembered for living outside the law and for being hunted by it, Morrison has impacted hip hop as an outlaw hero and a touchstone for those who work in the tradition of prophetic and poetic verse. His take on the subject of power, his credibility as a street poet, and some of the Doors' deep grooves have woven their way unexpectedly into contemporary rebel music. Hip hop's fantastical stories, often born of urban legend and rooted in folk and oral tradition are tied closely to the blues and its roots of rock'n'soul. While some of hip hop's wide variety of artists seek to shine a light on societal ills and gently correct them, others are overtly political, while there are those who play it wild and loose: Whatever the rap, hip hop's artists and its craft have a way of stirring controversy and making audiences uncomfortable, especially those who are outside the generations, races, and classes who predominantly enjoy it.

If it is unquestionably a purpose of art to pose questions, without always providing answers, hip hop as a nation is the ultimate trickster, running the spectrum as it does from embracing alternative lifestyles, to being the mainstream, a multi-billion dollar entertainment conglomerate and enterprise. Morrison and the Doors had of course confronted that same dichotomy, living through the rise in the '60s counterculture and watching as it was ultimately co-opted by industry. But a less detectable parallel is the way Morrison and the Doors' music have snuck in and left an imprint on hip hop's grooves: It is the band's stealth legacy.

The Cactus Album by 3rd Bass was first to use samples of "Peace Frog" and *An American Prayer* for its Bomb Squad-produced tracks in 1989, still early days in what would become sampling wars – the struggle for rightful permissions and licenses to use previously recorded, copyrighted material. The living Doors have since remained notoriously uptight about approving samples and are among the few hold-outs when it comes to lending their music for use in advertising.

"You know a long time ago, Jim Morrison kinda blew up at us, because we were *considering*, 'C'mon Buick, light my fire.'... Because the dough looked good and we were young. And Jim didn't primarily write that song, and I thought God, he cares about the catalog, what we represent in general, the whole thing. And he's dead. And I'm not. So I'm not gonna forget that," said Densmore.

Though you won't hear them often, Morrison's vocal tracks and the Doors' sounds have turned up in some unpredictable places through the years. For example, original West Coast gangsta rapper Snoop Dogg cut a version of "Riders on the Storm" for an electronic game. Speaking directly to Jim's ghost in the narrative, Snoop says, "Tell your story, you know the one I like," as he riffs on the line, "like a dog without a bone." The d-o double-g's version rides on imagery conjured by his crooning, LA street-style, with the "Lizard King bumping in the back."

In 2012, Frankie P mashed up a stash of Doors tracks with raps by Neptunes' protégés, Pusha T and Malice, better known as the Clipse, (from Florida). Conceived by Christopher B, and titled *Keys Open Doors*, Frankie P combined "Back Door Man," with the Clipse' own

"Funeral"; "Crawling King Snake," is paired with "Kinda Like a Big Deal," featuring an appearance by Kanye West.

"I know Kanye is a huge Jim Morrison fan," says producer Frankie P. "You can tell by his energy onstage and the fact he sampled 'Five to One' for Jay-Z's 'Takeover.' If you listen close you'll hear Jim ad-libbing in the background."[6]

In 2001 Morrison and the Doors made a massive leap into hip hop consciousness when producer Kanye West plucked a sample of "Five to One" as the music bed for "Takeover." The phrase "Five to One," was once thought to refer to the ratio of black casualties to white, during the war in Vietnam. The line, "They got guns but we got the numbers" sprung from a philosophical conversation between film school friends Morrison, Ray Manzarek, and Alain Ronay, debating the nature of revolution. The verse contains what became an often-repeated catchphrase associated with the Doors: "no one here gets out alive." The line, "Trading your hours for a handful of dimes" is just another one of Morrison's truisms behind the so-called American dream. And Densmore's strict timing evokes militaristic tension even before Morrison explodes into his "grhar..come on!" That rebellious yell roars throughout West and Jay-Z's track, conceived as a diss of fellow rapper, Nas. The piece launched a rap battle royale, but the sample almost didn't get cleared.

"I'm the main spoiler in that area," admits John Densmore, who's done his best to maintain the integrity of the catalog. Against the odds, West and Jay-Z were granted usage well before they were household names and hip hop dominators.

"Jay-Z asked us to sample 'Five to One' on 'Takeover.' Hip hop/rap was just coming up and I was like, 'what is this misogynist, bling stuff?' remembered Densmore who appears to have snoozed during hip hop's first 20 years. "He sent me a t-shirt, a basketball jersey, with Roc-A-Fella, and a letter, explaining how what they were trying to do was what we were trying to do in the '60s, talk about social change, and I went, 'Wow.' I got educated."[7]

As self-appointed guardian of the Doors' music and protector of it from commercial uses in the name of Morrison's wishes, Densmore's approval of "Takeover," was rife with contradictions. To begin, the multi-platinum successes of Jay-Z and Kanye West and their personal interests versus commitment to social good remain debatable. Their reputations and lifestyles as entrepreneurial hip hop moguls are the embodiment of the American spirit of materialism. Only a fraction of the population, approximately one percent, will ever see the kind of wealth West and Jay-Z enjoy, supplemented by the consumer tabloid press coverage of their relationships (with wives Kim Kardashian and Beyonce Knowles and the products they create and endorse).

Further confusing matters, as an artist and producer, West is known to freely cross boundaries between genres and to meld political and personal concerns alongside fanciful, as well as controversial themes (i.e. luxury rap in the age of austerity). His erratic, unhinged artistic streak is as appreciated by as many as are appalled by it. Following his infamous remarks (about President Bush's disregard for black lives) at the 2005 Concert for Katrina, and again in 2009 at the MTV Video Music Awards when he rushed the stage, West's behaviors prompted commentary from two sitting Presidents. Bush went as far as to say West's remarks were the "most disgusting moment" of his presidency (a period which included the events of 9/11 among other low points on the his watch, completed in 2009). Perhaps more a statement about the state of American culture than the artists, there was a time when an American president would not deign to comment on the behavior of a recording artist. Yet in recent years, Jay-Z was famously listed among the artists on President Obama's iPod and is counted among his personal friends.

Finally, West is also listed as producer of "The Rape Over," Mos Def's answerback to "Takeover." Calling out the hyper-consumer culture and hip hop as an industry, with the kind of inflammatory language for which hip hop is most often criticized, Mos Def (aka artist and activist Yasmin Bey) and his appropriation are arguably more in the spirit of Morrison and his anti-establishment, anti-war tirade, "Five to One," than Jay-Z and West's "Takeover." Yet without Morrison's conversation about Vietnam with his fellow film students there would be no "Five to One," no "Takeover," no "The Rape Over." Without "I'm Your Hoochie Coochie Man," there would have been no "Who Do you Love;" without Brando in *The Fugitive Kind*, '50s rocker Gene Vincent and Andy Warhol's Factory dancer, Gerard Malanga, there would have been no snakeskin pants for Jim, or any other rock stars in leather. Just as he participated in his own analog version of sampling – from Rimbaud, Céline, Brecht and Blake – the journey of "Five to One" not only illustrates the legacy of art that is groundbreaking and steeped in appropriation, but the trajectory of our accelerated lives and times. History repeats, reinvents, and life rolls on in a remix culture that in many ways Morrison predicted, though not all the developments are easily reconcilable.

In 2012 the three living Doors collaborated with electronic music DJ Skrillex. The LA phenomenon creates his tracks working entirely on a laptop – the young man with tapes and electronics Morrison envisioned – while the three Doors played along to his creation, "Breakin' a Sweat" (unrecognizable as bearing any relationship to the Doors and their music). The same year, New Orleans rapper Curren$y titled his album *The Stoned Immaculate*, after a line in Morrison's poem (and from "The WASP") in an effort to pay respect to Morrison, and to deliver the messages that helped him to an audience he believes would otherwise not have exposure to The Doors.

"'The End.' That's the first song I listen to every time that I listen to their music," he explains. "Sometimes I think a lot about what happens when you're not here. And that song kinda makes me feel like he's kinda doing the same thing. And just facing it, because there's really nothing you can do about it. So just to hear somebody deal with it and I know I'm not the only person to deal with it...."[8]

TechN9ne from Kansas City collaborated with the living Doors at Village Recorders in 2012. "I was in Jim's spot. When I was recording, they were watching me through the window." Originally set to cut " 'People Are Strange,' "It was Robby who suggested we do 'Strange Days,'" he said. For the rapper who named his label Strange Music and made a pilgrimage to Père Lachaise; "The experience of working with the Doors was the best ever, man."[9]

Morrison is a link from the '60s to the 21st Century's boundary busters of hip hop, though he may seem an unlikely choice as touchstone for a new generation of poet performers. Hip hop artists under 30 are also often judged harshly for their words and performances and pursued by law enforcement in a way that the previous generation's earliest rap stars were not. In the case of Tyler the Creator (of hip hop collective Odd Future/OFWGKTA) "allegedly inciting a riot"[10] was his crime in Texas in early 2014, his stage show perceived as a threat to law and order much like the Doors and rock 'n' roll were banned in the Bible Belt in their day.

Like Morrison, erratic behaviors and substance use and abuse may or may not play a role in the stories (but when they do, the condition is often accelerated by residual childhood stressors and systemic pressures). As the performer blurs lines between personal and public persona, the walls of protection fall and the stakes become higher. Potent words and a presence perceived threatening to authority are the common bonds, then and now.

A walk along Venice boardwalk in Los Angeles reveals two dominant images staring back from the tawdry t-shirt and poster shops: The faces of poets Tupac Shakur and Jim Morrison are rivaled only by products featuring Bob Marley and Al Pacino's fictional *Scarface* character, Tony Montana. The images of 2Pac and Mr. Mojo Risin' ensure the pair are very much alive on the streets of Venice; they serve as constant reminders of their words that aspired to illuminate and inspire, and of their lives, lived on the edge of darkness.

Beyond Hip Hop

As for the Doors and Morrison's personal legacy, Pamela Courson, the sole heir of Jim Morrison's estate, died in 1974; her inheritance was passed on to her family, a disposition the Morrison family famously contested and lost (though they retained music rights).

In 2000, a project titled *The Stoned Immaculate* organized by Elektra Records found the living Doors collaborating with a widely varied cast of contemporary musicians and fans from Perry Farrell and Exene to the Cult. Beyond Morrison's wildest dreams, studio voodoo has him sharing tracks with heroes Bo Diddley and John Lee Hooker and Beat writer William Burroughs who reads the lines, *Is everybody in? The ceremony's about to begin.*

In 2004, author Stephen Davis' Morrison biography *Jim Morrison: Life, Death, Legend* brought new information to the story of the singer and poet's final days in Paris, and it is from his account, along with Alain Ronay's first-hand telling and poet Ed Sanders' writing, that most latter-day information on Morrison has been drawn.

In 2005, after decades of silence, Morrison's great, lost love, Mary Werbelow, agreed to be interviewed by the *Tampa Bay Times*. Living in California at the time, she asserted it was the first and last time she wished to speak on the record about her relationship with Morrison.

Admiral Steve Morrison ultimately came to accept his son and his legacy and made peace with him. He upgraded the gravesite at Père Lachaise with the new plaque and a Greek inscription, meant to impart the sentiment that Morrison died as he lived, according to his own spirit. He passed away in 2008.

In 2010, Florida Governor Charlie Crist pardoned Morrison of all alleged wrongdoings from the Dade County stage, when after 40 years, still no evidence or eyewitnesses had ever confirmed there was any act of indecent exposure committed at the concert in Miami.

The living Doors celebrated the 40th anniversary of *LA Woman* in the fall of 2011 with a special reissue, shortly after proclaiming 2012 to be *The Year of The Doors*. Manzarek enjoyed a solo career and ultimately returned to playing the blues with Roy Rogers, the sideman, friend, and producer of John Lee Hooker. "It's definitely blues-based. It's 12-bar blues but with an expanded structure," said Manzarek. He and Krieger also played on the road with their version of the Doors. The pair appeared at the Sunset Strip Music festival, in conjunction with an exhibit of Henry Diltz's *Morrison Hotel* photos at the Standard, Hollywood's latest version of a party-til-you-die hotel, in the mold of the Hyatt on Sunset and the Chateau Marmont.

All of the above were ventures from which John Densmore opted out: Pursuing other interests from acting to activism, he's more likely to be found participating in the "world's biggest drum circle," part of a university music department's experiment in sound vibration, conducted with Grateful Dead drummer, Mickey Hart. Densmore was also a visible participant in the Occupy Wall Street movement, its core concern of income disparity and a general wish toward creating economic justice for all. He also penned two versions of his Doors stories, both published; the second volume, *The Doors: Unhinged* recounts his legal battle with the band over the use of its name and serves as a larger meditation on greed. Ultimately it was Densmore who adopted Morrison's mystical and shamanistic interests in music's ability to heal, alongside his other esoteric interests outside the popular culture.

On May 20, 2013, Ray Manzarek passed away in Germany while undergoing treatment for bile duct cancer. Survived by his wife Dorothy and son Pablo, his surviving bandmates, Kreiger and Densmore, ended their longstanding feud and announced plans to perform and record again.

In his memoir, Manzarek wrote of his recurring dream about Jim and the Doors making music again, "But every once in a while he tries to float away, carried off by the inspiration, into the blue canopy, off into the light. But I bring him back with a firm hand on his ankle and a cool blues line on the organ. And he's grounded again."[11]

In a world ripe for change and in a state of disrepair, Jim Morrison's words ring loud and clear:

What have we done to the earth?
What have we done to our fair sister?

It is a fair question. Environmental terror is very much with us in the age of climate change: Unceasing militarism and corporate greed have done their share to endanger people and the planet. Other matters which concerned youth in the '60s, from racial and gender equality to police brutality, are alarmingly still here, but the student population and millennial generation is once again rising and mobilizing, even in the face of increased surveillance and risk. These conscious and conscientious objectors recognize that what is happening environmentally and economically – that a few should thrive while the majority suffers – is not only unsustainable, it is wrong.

"You have to be in a constant state of revolution or you're dead," once said Jim Morrison. "If my poetry aims to achieve anything, it's to deliver people from the limited ways in which they see and feel."[11]

At the end of 2013, Graham Nash sold at auction one of Jim Morrison's notebooks, a gift to the singer from their shared manager Bill Siddons. Described in the catalog as Morrison's "Paris" notebook, the book in fact dates back to Morrison's early '60s student days. Taped on the inside, there is a picture of artist Francis Bacon and some handwritten quotes, as in this one from Norman Mailer: "Sometimes I feel as if there's a vast guerrilla war going on for the mind of man, communist against communist, capitalist against capitalist, artist against artist. And the stakes are huge. Will we spoil the best secrets of life or will we help to free a new kind of man? It's intoxicating to think of that. There's something rich waiting, if one of us is brave enough and good enough to get there."[13]

There are also fragments of Morrison's own writings scattered throughout.

A man searching
for lost paradise
can seem a fool
to those who never
sought the other world

Had he lived and continued to work and recover from his demons, in all likelihood Morrison would take his place alongside Bob Dylan, Lou Reed, and Leonard Cohen at the table of rock's literary giants. As it was, he became something else: Eternal. Over seven studio albums by the Doors, six in his lifetime and a final one posthumously, on which his voice is central, Morrison remains very much a vital force in rock. His palm trees of Venice, his bloody red sun and fantastic LA are a light in the dark night of the American city and its soul. From the break of dawn until the end of the night, the urban sprawl hisses, like a snake threatening to swallow its people whole. But there's salvation in the songs, in Morrison's words. Blowing through the canyons, whistling across the beaches and through the windows of every little bungalow – they are in the air there. Burning bright as Blake's tiger, a bonfire at the beach or on Skid Row, Jim Morrison's words are writ across the night bold as they ever were. Take a ride on a moonlight drive, and hear his appeal howl: *Save our city. Right now.*

ACKNOWLEDGMENTS

The author wishes to thank Kent Gustavson, Mary Sellers, Megan DeWeerdt, and all at Sumach-Red/Blooming Twig Books for the opportunity and experience on the new frontier of publishing; Barbara Stauffacher Solomon and Laurie Sheets Forbes for cover design; David Ensminger and Lisa McElroy for editorial consult; Frank Reiss, Jennifer Joseph, Tyson Cornell, Tosh Berman and Yuval Taylor for publishing expertise, and especially Deirdre Greene for her initial interest in the project. Thanks to the Cities of Los Angeles and Santa Monica for inspiration, Jim Morrison and the Doors for the soundtrack, and to my friends, family, and colleagues for enthusiasm and support, especially: Jack Boulware and Litquake, Linda Butler, Jim Cherry, Charles R. Cross, Jeff and Jess Finn, Lisa Freeman and Phranc Gottlieb, Fred Mills, Nellie King Solomon, Victor Krummenacher, Layne Sterling, Wendy Wall, and most of all my husband and one true love, Peter Case.

Notes

Chapter 1

This is the End: 1964-1965

1. Ray Manzarek, *Light My Fire*, (New York: Penguin, 1999), 53.
2. IBID
3. IBID
4. IBID, 74.
5. Robert Farley, "Mary and Jim to the End," *St. Petersburg Times*, September 25, 2005 http://www.sptimes.com/2005/09/25/Doors/Mary_and_Jim_to_the_e.shtml. This is the one and only interview with Mary Werbelow, Morrison's pre-Doors girlfriend and post-Doors confidante of longstanding. Farley's additional interviews with Jim's friends in Clearwater made a major contribution in the movement to reexamine Morrison's stature as an artist, a legacy that stands in contrast to the rock star legend.
6. Wallace Fowlie, *Rimbaud and Jim Morrison: The Rebel As Poet, A Memoir*, (Durham, NC and London: Duke University Press, 1993). Fowlie, a professor of French literature, author, and translator, was the first to publish a serious consideration of Morrison's work as a poet of the ages.

Chapter 2: Santa Monica, Venice, and The Doors of Perception: 1965-1966

1. Interviews with Philomene Long and Frank T. Rios from the DVD *Venice West and the LA Scene*, Mary Kerr, Director, 2011, CA

Palm. A great in-depth look at the Venice Beat Era that preceded the Doors' arrival to the area.

2. Jerry Hopkins, "The Rolling Stone Interview: Jim Morrison," *Rolling Stone*, July 26, 1969, 15.

3. Jac Holzman, Gawan Davis, *Follow the Music: The Life and High Times of Elektra Records in the Great Years of American Pop Culture* (First Media, 1998), 160.

4. John Densmore, *My Life With Jim Morrison and The Doors* (Random House, New York, 2009).

5. Jim Morrison, *The Lost Writings of Jim Morrison, Wilderness Volume 1*, (Vintage, New York, 1988), 2.
6. Robert Farley, "Mary and Jim to the End," *St. Petersburg Times*, September 25, 2005 http://www.sptimes.com/2005/09/25/Doors/Mary_and_Jim_to_the_e.shtml.

Chapter 3

Sunset Strip: 1966-1967

1. Ray Manzarek, *Light My Fire*, (New York: Penguin, 1999).

2. John Einerson, *Forever Changes, Arthur Lee and the Book of Love*, (London: Jawbone, 2010), 144.

3. IBID, 124

4. Edward Sanders, "Woodstock Journal, The Final Times of Jim Morrison" http://www.woodstockjournal.com/pdf/Morrison%27sFinalMonths.pdf retrieved, October 2013.
5. Jac Holzman, Gawan Davis, *Follow the Music: The Life and High Times of Elektra Records in the Great Years of American Pop Culture* (First Media, 1998).
6. Blair Jackson, interview with Paul Rothchild, *BAM*, July 3, 1981 archived http://archives.waiting-forthe-sun.net/Pages/Interviews/OtherInterviews/rothchild_bam.html retrieved January 2013.

7. Einerson, *Forever Changes, Arthur Lee and the Book of Love*, 144.

8. Paul Williams *The Crawdaddy! Book*, (New York, Hal Leonard, 2002), 171.

9. Jerry Hopkins, "The Rolling Stone Interview: Jim Morrison," *Rolling Stone*, July 26, 1969, 16.

10. Bill Moyers, *Joseph Campbell and the Power of Myth – The Heroes Adventure*, 1988 http://billmoyers.com/content/ep-1-joseph-campbell-and-the-power-of-myth-the-hero's-adventure-audio/.

11. Northrop Frye, *Fearful Symmetry A Study of William Blake*, (Princeton: University Press, 1969),135.

Chapter 4

Strange Days Have Found Him: 1967

1. Paul Williams, *The Crawdaddy! Book*, (Milwaukee: Hal Leonard, 2002, 1967), 166-170.

2. Jerry Hopkins, "The Rolling Stone Interview: Jim Morrison," *Rolling Stone*, July 26, 1969, Rolling Stone archives.

3. Robert Farley, "Mary and Jim to the End," *St. Petersburg Times*, September 25, 2005 http://www.sptimes.com/2005/09/25/Doors/Mary_and_Jim_to_the_e.shtml.

4. Various online resources and local history groups contributed to this patchwork history of Southern California's beaches and piers. Santa Monica History Museum, 1350 7th Street in Santa Monica (and online at http://santamonicahistory.org) is a good starting point.

5. The Doors chronological history http://doorshistory.com served as the source for tour dates and concert attendance figures.

Chapter 5

Shaman's Blues: 1968

1. Jerry Hopkins, "The Rolling Stone Interview: Jim Morrison," *Rolling Stone*, July 26, 1969, Rolling Stone archives.

2. Barbara Charone, "Ray Manzarek Opens a New Door," *Rolling Stone*, August 15, 1974, 24.

3. Ray Manzarek, *Light My Fire*, (New York: Penguin, 1999), 288.

4. John Einerson, *Forever Changes, Arthur Lee and the Book of Love*, (London: Jawbone, 2010), 125. Stories regarding Morrison's transgressions while under the influence range from hard to believe (but true) to apocryphal and were offensive to people across the board. Arthur Lee details one such event. There are more.

5. Canter's Deli history http://www.cantersdeli.com/history.html

6. Jerrold Greenberg, "Butterfield on Rock Blues: I Can't Believe The Doors," *Rolling Stone*, April 6, 1968.

7. Blair Jackson, interview with Paul Rothchild, *BAM*, July 3, 1981 archived http://archives.waiting-forthe-sun.net/Pages/Interviews/OtherInterviews/rothchild_bam.html retrieved January 2013.

8. Hopkins, "The Rolling Stone Interview: Jim Morrison."

9. Rainer Moddemann, Robby Krieger interview http://www.reocities.com/SunsetStrip/Palladium/1409/robby.htm,retrieved February 2014

10. Manzarek, *Light My Fire*.

11. Manzarek, *Light My Fire*.

12. Jac Holzman, Gawan Davis, *Follow the Music: The Life and High Times of Elektra Records in the Great Years of American Pop Culture* (First Media, 1998), 289.

13. Richard Goldstein, interview with the Doors, PBS *Critique*, 1969.

14. Hopkins, "The Rolling Stone Interview: Jim Morrison."

15. Howard Smith, *Village Voice* interview with Jim Morrison, November 6, 1969, raw tape retrieved 2012: http://www.youtube.com/watch?v=2Dgc8D7CTao

16. Harlan Lane, *The Wild Boy of Aveyron* (Cambridge, Harvard University Press, 1976). A fairly modern take on Itard's 19th Century findings, but far from an up-to-date resource on treating speech and hearing impaired children in the post-technology era.

17. Robert Farley, "Mary and Jim to the End," *St. Petersburg Times*, September 25, 2005 http://www.sptimes.com/2005/09/25/Doors/Mary_and_Jim_to_the_e.shtml

Chapter 6

Paradise Lost: 1969

1. Televised interview with Morrison outside Miami courtroom. Courtesy Louis Wolfson II Florida Moving Image Archive. Retrieved October 27, 2013 http://www.youtube.com/watch?v=4Ap2GNPsXPM

2. John Tytell, *The Living Theater, Art, Exile and Outrage*, (New York, Grove Press, 1997).

3. Ray Manzarek, *Light My Fire*, (New York: Penguin, 1999).

4. William James, *The Essential Writings* edited by Bruce W. Wilshire, (New York: SUNY Press, 1984), 125. Additional information on alcoholism: Robert M. Morse, MD, Danile K. Flavin, MD, "The Definition of Alcoholism," JAMA Journal of the American Medical

Association, August 26, 1992. Retrieved December, 2013 http://jama.jamanetwork.com/article.aspx?articleid=399449

5. Allen Ginsberg, *Spontaneous Mind Selected Interviews 1958-1996*, David Carter, editor (New York: Harper Collins, 2001).

6. *Alcoholics Anonymous*, New York: AA World Services, 1939 & 2001.

7. Howard Smith, *Village Voice* interview with Jim Morrison, November 6, 1969, Doors office Los Angeles, raw tape retrieved 2012: http://www.youtube.com/watch?v=2Dgc8D7CTao.

8. Ben Fong-Torres, "Back to the Bible for Californians," *Rolling Stone*, July 12, 1969. Miltowns are the brand name of a tranquilizing drug frequently prescribed to women of the '50s, '60s and '70s, ostensibly for relief from the tension of homemaking.

9. Unfortunately Morrison never had a chance to record in Spanish, despite his interest in the Americas' indigenous people and his residencies in both Florida and California. Jim Morrison and the Doors remain giants in Spanish-speaking countries.

10. Smith, *Village Voice* interview with Jim Morrison.

11. Richard Goldstein, interview with the Doors, 1969, PBS *Critique*.

12. Carla De Santis Black "Rock Chick: An Interview with Patricia Kennealy Morrison" *Meow* online, Sept. 13 2013 retrieved September 13, 2013

http://meowonline.org/rock-chick-an-interview-with-patricia-kennealy-morrison/

13. Paul Garon, *Blues and the Poetic Spirit* (San Francisco: City Lights, 1996), 54.

Chapter 7

Back to Basics: 1969-1970

1. Jerry Hopkins, "The Rolling Stone Interview: Jim Morrison," *Rolling Stone*, July 26, 1969, Rolling Stone archives.

2. IBID

3. "Photographer Henry Diltz Presents Classics Shots of The Doors at the Standard Hotel" *Huffington Post*, August 15, 2012, retrieved August 15, 2012 http://www.huffingtonpost.com/2012/08/15/photographer-henry-diltz-_n_1773339.html?1345032637&utm_hp_ref=arts.

4. Additional statistics and the general conditions of Skid Row were gleaned from the author's firsthand observations, *Los Angeles Times* coverage and the consistent reporting of Patt Morrison, like this broadcast: "Why is LA Still the Homeless Capital of the Nation?" KPCC, January 26, 2011 http://www.scpr.org/news/2011/01/26/23403/patt-morrison-why-la-still-homeless-capital-nation/.

4. Hopkins, "The Rolling Stone Interview: Jim Morrison"

5. Howard Smith, *Village Voice* interview with Jim Morrison, November 6, 1969, Doors office Los Angeles, raw tape retrieved 2012: http://www.youtube.com/watch?v=2Dgc8D7CTao.

6. Hopkins, "The Rolling Stone Interview: Jim Morrison."

7. Jim Morrison interview, source unidentified, September 5, 1970, San Diego, CA http://www.youtube.com/watch?v=iQgccjhLjYE retrieved February 2014.

8. Smith, *Village Voice* interview with Jim Morrison.

9. Jim Morrison Miami Trial 1970 footage https://www.youtube.com/watch?v=iPAKy6rAqTg
retrieved

Chapter 8

LA Women: 1970-1971

1. All quotes from Jim Morrison in the early portion of the chapter are from the an audio interview with John Tobler of *Zig Zag* magazine, conducted backstage at the 1970 Isle of Wight http://www.youtube.com/watch?v=T8WUlJKN_Xc&list=RDT8WUlJKN_Xc retrieved 2013.

2. Jac Holzman, Gawan Davis, *Follow the Music: The Life and High Times of Elektra Records in the Great Years of American Pop Culture* (First Media, 1998).

3. Alan Paul, "Interview: Robby Krieger The Doors' Guitarist Discusses Some of the Best Tracks on Reissued LA Woman Album" Guitarworld May 7, 2012 retrieved May 7, 2012 http://www.guitarworld.com/interview-doors-robby-krieger-discusses-some-best-tracks-reissued-la-woman-album

4. Audio interview with Ben Fong-Torres of *Rolling Stone*, conducted at Norton apartment complex, February 1971. retrieved from You Tube, October 2012. http://www.youtube.com/watch?v=VCS_aVuuPdg

5. Paul, "Interview:Robby Krieger"

Chapter 9

Au Revoir LA: 1971

1. Martin R. Smith, *Doors Mr. Mojo Risin' The Story of L.A. Woman*, DVD, Eagle Vision/Doors Property LLC, 2011.

2. Alain Ronay "Jim and I – Friends Until Death" originally published in King & I, 2002, retrieved in 2012 from http://archives.waiting-forthe-sun.net/Pages/Articles/jims_last_days.html

3. Martin R. Smith, *Doors Mr. Mojo Risin' The Story of L.A. Woman*

4. John Densmore, *My Life With Jim Morrison and The Doors* (Random House, New York, 2009).

5. IBID. The Golden Bear was a nightclub in Huntington Beach, California where rock, folk and blues acts played from the '50s until it closed in the '80s.

6. Ray Manzarek, *Light My Fire*, (New York: Penguin, 1999).

Chapter 10

Since Then: 1971-2013

1. Jim Morrison interviewed on PBS *Critique*, 1969, video clip, http://www.youtube.com/watch?v=-1PSalLKmD0Retrieved from youtube, 2012.

2. *CBS This Morning*, Patti Smith interview http://www.youtube.com/watch?v=hj48Y3Ik-Gg retrieved April 1 2012.

3. Simon Hattenstone, "Patti Smith: punk poet queen," *The Guardian*, May 24, 2013 Retrieved May 24, 2013 http://www.theguardian.com/music/2013/may/25/patti-smith-interview-punk-poet

4. Paul Trynka, *Open Up And Bleed*, (New York: Three Rivers Press, 2008),69.

5. Mark Spitz and Brendan Mullen, *We Got the Neutron Bomb. The Untold Story of LA Punk* (New York: Three Rivers Press, 2001), 4.

6. Phillip Mlynar, "Clipse and The Doors, Together at Last" http://www.mtvhive.com/2012/03/29/clipse-the-doors-mash-up/ retrieved, March 29, 2012

7. John Densmore "The Doors' Talk 'Regeneration' and Working With Skrillex." http://www.youtube.com/watch?v=Qxr-XliiJ9E retrieved February 27, 2014.

8. Georgette Klein, "In House With Curren$y: Rapper Shares The Doors Inspiration, Wiz Khalifa Sessions, Album Memories," July 24, 2012, retrieved July 24, 2012 http://theboombox.com/currensy-the-stoned-immaculate/

9. http://www.rollingstone.com/music/news/tyler-the-creator-arrested-at-sxsw-20140315 retrieved March 26, 2014

10. "TechN9ne Talks of Becoming Next Diddy, Colab with Jim Morrison" http://www.youtube.com/watch?v=zyDrWj89Les, "Behind the Scenes The Making of Tech N9ne's Strange Days." http://www.youtube.com/watch?v=Vz5jT1RSHLg

11. Ray Manzarek, *Light My Fire*, (New York: Penguin, 1999), 350-351.

12. Jim Morrison, *The Lost Writings of Jim Morrison, Wilderness Vol. 1*, (New York: Vintage Books, 1988), 2.

13. Steven Marcus, The Art of Fiction No. 32, Norman Mailer, *The Paris Review*, Winter-Spring 1964. Retrieved March 27, 2014. http://www.theparisreview.org/interviews/4503/the-art-of-fiction-no-32-norman-mailer

Bibliography

Algren, Nelson. *Chicago City on the Make*, The University of Chicago Press, 2001.

Bergan, Ronald, editor. *François Truffaut Interviews*, University Press of Mississippi, 2008.

Brecht, Bertolt. *The Threepenny Opera,* Grove Press, 1960.

Davis, Stephen. *Jim Morrison: Life, Death, Legend*, Gotham Books, 2004.

Densmore, John. *Riders on the Storm: My Life with Jim Morrison and The Doors*, Delacorte Press, 1990.

Didion, Joan. *The White Album,* Simon & Schuster, 1979.

Einerson, John. *Arthur Lee and the Book of Love.* London: Jawbone, 2010.

Fong-Torres, Ben. *The Doors*, Hyperion, 2006.

Fowlie, Wallace. *Rimbaud and Jim Morrison The Rebel as Poet a Memoir*, Duke University Press, 1993.

Ginsberg, Allen. *Spontaneous Mind Selected Interviews 1958-1996*, Harper Collins, 2001.

Graves, Robert. *The White Goddess A Historical Grammar of Poetic Myth*, Farrar Straus Giroux, 1948.

Lee, Martin A. and Shlain, Bruce. *Acid Dreams The Complete Social History of LSD: The CIA, The Sixties, And Beyond*, Grove Press, 1985.

Manzarek, Ray. *Light My Fire* by Ray Manzarek, New York: G.P. Putnum's Sons, 1988.

Morrison, Jim. *The Lords and the New Creatures*, Touchstone, 1971.

Morrison, Jim. *Wilderness: The Lost Writings of Jim Morrison*, Vol. 1. New York: Vintage Books, 1989.

Morrison, Jim. *American Night: The Writings of Jim Morrison*, Vol. 2. New York: Vintage Books, 1991.

Rechy, John, *City of Night*, Grove Press, 1963.

Rochlin, Michael Jacob. *Ancient LA And Other Essays*, Unreinforced Masonry Studio, 1999.

Smith, Patti. *Just Kids*, Ecco, 2010.

Spitz, Mark and Mullen, Brendan. *We Got the Neutron Bomb The Untold Story of LA Punk*, Three Rivers Press, 2001.

Starr, Kevin. *Coast of Dreams California on the Edge*, 1990-2003, Alfred A. Knopf, 2004.

Starr, Kevin, *California: A History*, Modern Library, 2007.

Sterrit, David. *Jean-Luc Godard Interviews,* University Press of Mississippi, 1998.

Sugarman, Danny. *The Doors: The Illustrated History*. New York: William Morrow and Company, 1983.

Trynka, Paul. *Open Up and Bleed*, Three Rivers Press, 1998.

Tytell, John. *The Living Theater*, Art Exile and Outrage Grove Press, 1997.

Williams, Paul. *The Crawdaddy Book: Writing and Images from the Magazine of Rock*, Hal Leonard, 2002.

Articles and Reviews

Aronowitz, Al. "This is the End, Beautiful Friend," *Melody Maker*, July 17, 1971, 15.

Bosco, Joe. Interview: Robby Krieger on The Doors LA Woman, Skrillex and Jim Morrison, *Music radar.com* Jan 29, 2012.

Cline, Georgette. "In House with Curren$y: Rapper Shares The Doors Inspiration," *Boombox*, July 24, 2012, http://the boombox.com/currensy-the-stoned-immaculate/.

Farley, Robert. "Mary and Jim to the End," *St. Petersburg Times*, September 25, 2005. http://www.sptimes.com/2005/09/25/Doors/Mary_and_Jim_to_the_e.shtml

Goldstein, Richard. "The Shaman as Superstar," *New York Magazine*, August 5, 1968, 42-45.

Greenberg, Jerrold. "Butterfield on Rock Blues: I can't believe the Doors" *Rolling Stone*, April 6, 1968,

Jackson, Blair. Interview with Paul Rothchild, *BAM*, July 3, 1981.

James, Lizze. Interview with Jim Morrison, Parts I & II, reprinted in *The Doors' Illustrated History*.

Mills, Fred. "Resting in Pieces," *Creative Loafing*, March 16, 1991, 3-4.

"The Doors: Reconciling the Man, the Myth and the Movie," *The Bob*, Issue 41, 1991, 31-34

Paul, Alan. Interview: The Doors' Robby Kreiger Discusses Some of the Best Tracks on Reissued 'LA Woman' Album, *Guitarworld.com*, May 7, 2012, retrieved 5/11/12/

http://www.guitarworld.com/interview-doors-robby-krieger-discusses-some-best-tracks-reissued-la-woman-album

Moddemann, Rainer. "Robby Kreiger interview" http://www.reocities.com/SunsetStrip/Palladium/1409/robby.htm Retrieved February 27, 2014.

"Interview with Jim Morrison and The Doors," *Hullaballoo*, October/November, 1968.

Audio, Video and DVD

Densmore, John. "The Doors' Talk 'Regeneration' and Working With Skrillex." http://www.youtube.com/watch?v=Qxr-XliiJ9E, retrieved July 5, 2012.

Fong-Torres, Ben. Jim Morrison, *Rolling Stone* interview,
raw audio recording, February 1971 http://www.youtube.com/watch?v=71-dR5go2KE

Justman, Paul, with Manzarek, Ray and Densmore, John. *The Doors Live In Europe* 1968, Eagle Vision, 2004.

Kerr, Mary. *Venice West and the LA Scene*, DVD CA Palm, 2011.

Smith, Howard. Jim Morison, *Village Voice* Interview with Howard Smith, retrieved April 2012

http://www.youtube.com/watch?v=temV0r_cJEg&feature=youtu.be

Smith, Martin R. Doors *Mr. Mojo Risin': The Story of LA Woman*, Eagle Vision, 2011

Smith, Patti. on Jim Morrison, *CBS This Morning*, retrieved April 1, 2012. http://www.youtube.com/watch?v=hj48Y3Ik-Gg

Index

A

"Alabama Song (Whisky Bar)" 25, 71, 79
Alameda, CA *ii, iv*
Albuquerque, NM *ii*
Alcoholics Anonymous 129, 198
alcoholism 36, 91, 99, 124, 125, 126, 128, 129, 150
Alta Cienega Motor Inn 71, 73, 96
An American Prayer 132, 174, 179
Artaud, Antonin 26, 30, 122
Astbury, Ian 176

B

"Back Door Man" 71, 111
Barney's Beanery 95, 96
Beck, Julian 121
"Been Down So Long" 160
Berkeley, CA 19, 20, 26
Berman, Wallace 38, 114
Bey, Yasmin 182
Blake, William 35, 43, 54, 61, 88, 135, 195
Bosch, Hieronymus 143
Botnick, Bruce 71, 72, 140, 159, 172
"Break on Through" 71, 75
Brecht, Bertolt 24, 30, 31
Brig, The 33, 122
Buñuel, Luis 27
Burdon, Eric 93

C

The Cactus Album 179
Cahiers du Cinema 33
Canned Heat 84, 89, 96, 98, 99, 100, 108, 113, 140, 155
Canter's Deli 96, 197
Céline, Louis-Ferdinand 41, 43, 69, 182
Cervenka, Exene 169, 175
Chateau Marmont 96, 186
Cheetah Club 76
Chumash people 44
cinéma vérité 107
City Lights Bookstore 13, 26
City of Night 58, 59, 90, 206
Clipse, The 179
COINTELPRO 149
Courson, Pamela 65, 66, 73, 124, 158, 166, 185
Crawdaddy! 75, 195, 211
"Crawling King Snake" 180
"Crystal Ship, The" 71
Cult, The 176, 185
Curren$y 183, 203, 207

D

Dade County, FL 123, 149, 186
Dali, Salvador 27
Densmore, John 51, 59, 66, 87, 165, 180, 186, 194
Diddley, Bo 84, 88, 103, 108, 185
Dietrich, Marlene 23
Dinner Keys Auditorium 119

Dixon, Willie 71, 104, 111, 144
Doe, John 175
Doors, The 40, 54, 55, 57, 58, 61, 63, 64, 65, 66, 68–94, 96, 97, 98, 102, 103, 106, 107, 108, 110, 112, 113, 114, 116, 117, 119, 122, 123, 125, 126, 127, 131, 132, 133, 134, 135, 139, 141, 145, 151, 154, 155, 156, 157, 158, 159, 163, 165, 166, 172, 173, 174, 175, 176, 177, 178, 179, 180, 181, 183, 184, 185, 186, 189, 191, 196

–formation 82

–musical style 39, 111, 134, 141, 154, 171, 172

–studio 54, 72, 79, 82, 93, 94, 101, 102, 106, 107, 113, 116, 137, 139, 156, 157, 158, 163, 165, 185, 189

–touring 67, 82, 90, 93, 124, 134, 145, 149, 156, 173

Doors of Perception, The 35, 50, 54, 194

E

Elektra Records 65, 69, 96, 158, 185, 194, 195, 197
Éluard, Paul 26, 168
"End, The" 18
"End of the Night" 43, 55, 69

F

FBI 85, 124, 149
Feast of Friends 107, 132, 134, 163
Ferlinghetti, Lawrence 13, 120
"Five to One" 177, 180, 182
Florida State University 17
Fong-Torres, Ben 132, 159, 199, 201
Fowlie, Wallace 28, 193
Frankie P 179, 180
Fujikawa, Dorothy 18, 26, 30, 31, 33, 40, 41, 44, 57, 58, 71, 106, 187

G

Genet, Jean 26, 121
Ginsberg, Allen 13, 59, 106, 120, 128, 198
Godard, Jean Luc 14, 24
"Go Insane" 55, 145

H

"Hello I Love You" 44
Hendrix, Jimi 55, 64, 79, 88, 93, 137, 150, 154, 155, 172, 177
hip hop 147, 178, 180, 181, 182, 183, 184, 185, 211
Hirschman, Jack 26, 114
Holzman, Jac 69, 146, 153, 159, 194, 195, 197
Hopkins, Jerry 132, 175, 194, 195, 196
"Horse Latitudes" 83
House UnAmerican Activities Committee 25
Howlin' Wolf *iii*, 53, 104
Huxley, Aldous 47, 48, 127

HWY: An American Pastoral 131, 174

I

"Indian Summer" 55, 140

J

Jacob, Max 26
Jakob, Dennis 37, 94
Jay-Z 180–182
Joplin, Janis 55, 88, 93, 137, 150, 155, 157, 172, 177
Journey to the End of the Night 41
Jung, Carl 73, 126

K

Kaleidoscope, The 96, 108
Kennealy, Patricia 135, 146, 199
Kerouac, Jack 35, 59, 121
Krieger, Robby 51, 55, 102, 134, 146, 150, 158, 165, 197

L

"La Bateau ivre" 28, 29
La Cienega 94, 96, 156
L.A. Woman 202
Lead Belly 111, 112
Lee, Arthur 64, 65, 69, 93, 154, 157, 194, 196, 197, 205
Lenya, Lotte 24, 25
Lewis, Furry 160
"Light My Fire" 58, 66, 78, 79, 81
Lisciandro, Frank 94, 131
Living Theater, The 120, 121, 122, 161, 198

Lizard King 106, 109, 115, 127, 151, 175, 179
London Fog, The 63, 64, 66, 68, 69, 154
Long, Philomene 38, 169, 194
Los Altos, CA *ii*
Los Angeles, CA *v*, 44, 45, 46, 51, 56, 58, 61, 64, 66, 85, 99, 117, 119, 121, 124, 155, 176, 184, 191
love *v*, 18, 19, 22, 27, 44, 50, 58, 59, 61, 87, 91, 100, 102, 103, 123, 126, 133, 134, 150, 176, 185, 191
"Love Me Two Times" 82, 175
LSD 37, 47, 50, 51, 54, 56, 70, 127, 128, 205

M

"Maggie M'Gill" 144
Mailer, Norman *iv*, 61, 132, 188, 204
Manzarek, Ray 18, 19, 23, 24, 26, 31, 32, 36, 40, 41, 43, 51, 54, 57, 64, 65, 66, 70, 83, 89, 93, 104, 107, 124, 125, 126, 141, 163, 166, 176, 177, 180, 186, 187, 193, 194, 196, 197, 198, 202, 204, 205, 208
Marriage of Heaven and Hell, The 54
McClure, Michael 114, 120, 121, 132, 164
Melbourne, FL *ii*

Miami, FL 119, 123, 131, 136, 145, 148, 149, 150, 155, 165, 186, 198, 201
"Moonlight Drive" 41, 44, 55, 57, 83, 85
Morrison, Admiral Stephen 30
Morrison, Andy *ii*
Morrison, Anne *ii*
Morrison, Clara *ii*
Morrison, Jim
    –arrests *v*, 63, 85, 91, 116, 119, 123, 124, 150
    –childhood 128, 184
    –drugs 20, 37, 39, 92, 107, 137, 158, 167, 176
    –family *i, ii, iv*, 17, 61, 91, 97, 124, 125, 128, 155
    –films *iv*, 18, 19, 22, 23, 31, 32, 33, 35, 36, 106, 107, 131, 134, 135, 141, 150, 163, 164, 174, 180, 182
    –friends *i, iii, iv*, 16, 17, 19, 36, 38, 39, 48, 50, 56, 63, 82, 84, 91, 92, 94, 95, 96, 107, 124, 131, 133, 146, 166, 167, 180, 182, 191, 193
    –notebooks 39, 61, 83, 188
    –poetry *ii, iii*, 17, 19, 29, 30, 33, 35, 36, 54, 59, 60, 61, 102, 104, 105, 106, 114, 122, 123, 130, 132, 135, 137, 163, 169, 171, 175, 188
    –songs *iii, iv*, 25, 29, 39, 41, 43, 44, 57, 60, 64, 65, 66, 71, 72, 76, 78, 83, 88, 90, 97, 99, 102, 104, 106, 110, 111, 112, 114, 122, 136, 139, 140, 144, 145, 158, 159, 161, 166, 189
    –substance abuse 92, 174
    –UCLA 17, 18, 19, 21, 22, 23, 24, 26, 31, 32, 33, 40, 43, 50, 51, 60, 99, 114, 122, 163
Morrison Hotel 55, 139, 140, 141, 144, 186
Morrison, Van 79
Mos Def 182
Mr. Mojo Risin' 115, 152, 159, 184, 202, 208

N

Neuwirth, Bob 107
Nouvelle vague 24

O

Oakland, CA *iii*, 52, 86

P

Paradise Lost 119, 133, 135, 137, 198
Paris 67, 158, 163, 164, 165, 166, 168, 185, 188, 204
"Peace Frog" *i*, 139, 179
"People Are Strange" 84, 183
Père Lachaise 164, 167, 168, 183, 185
Pop, Iggy 173, 174

Q

Queneau, Raymond 26

R

Rechy, John 59, 206
Redding, Otis 55, 110, 111, 112, 113

Renoir, Jean 24
Reverdy, Pierre 26
"Riders on the Storm" 51, 160, 161, 163, 165, 179, 205
Rimbaud, Arthur *v*, 28, 29, 30, 41, 59, 61, 88, 172, 182, 193, 205
"Roadhouse Blues" 98, 101, 144, 145
Rolling Stone 39, 85, 86, 89, 110, 122, 126, 132, 134, 136, 144, 145, 158, 175, 194, 195, 196, 197, 199, 200, 201, 207, 208, 215
Ronay, Alain 94, 164, 167, 180, 185, 202
Rothchild, Paul 70, 71, 72, 74, 102, 106, 109, 140, 145, 155, 156, 157, 158, 195, 197, 207
Rue Beautreillis 163
"Runnin' Blue" 108, 110, 111, 112

S

San Francisco, CA *iii*, 26, 45, 48, 51, 78, 80, 114, 121, 144, 199, 215
Santa Monica, CA 21, 25, 35, 37, 40, 41, 42, 43, 49, 51, 56, 57, 59, 61, 76, 77, 82, 94, 95, 96, 100, 112, 170, 191, 194, 196
Sea Witch, The 63
shaman 44, 109, 120, 131, 164
"Shaman's Blues" *iii, iv*, 87, 110, 113, 115, 116, 117, 196
"Ship of Fools" 143, 144
Smith, Howard 133, 147, 150, 161, 197, 199, 200, 208

Smith, Patti 172, 203
Snoop Dogg 179
Soft Parade, The 109, 110, 111, 112, 114, 116, 119, 134, 135, 169
"Soul Kitchen" 60, 89, 175, 176
Stanley, Owsley 51
Stone Temple Pilots 176
Strange Days 55, 75, 79, 81, 83, 84, 85, 93, 101, 183, 195, 203
Sugerman, Danny 175
"Summer's Almost Gone" 41, 43, 55, 102
Sunset Strip 53, 54, 60, 63, 64, 65, 67, 71, 73, 88, 89, 132, 174, 186, 194

T

"Take It As It Comes" 72
"Takeover" 177, 180, 181, 182
Theater of Cruelty 27, 114, 161
3rd Bass 179
Topanga Canyon 54, 96, 98, 100, 155
Topanga Corral 98, 100, 101
Touch Me 110, 115, 116
Truffaut, François 24, 115, 205

U

Un Chien Andalou 27
Une Saison en enfer 29
"Unknown Soldier, The" 106

V

Varda, Agnes 24, 167
Venice, CA 21, 33, 35, 36, 37, 38, 39, 40, 41, 42, 43, 58, 59, 60, 61, 63, 65, 68, 77, 94, 100, 111, 112, 139,

141, 154, 163, 168, 169, 170, 172, 175, 184, 189, 194, 208
Victor of Aveyron 115
Village Voice 134, 146, 148, 161, 197, 199, 200, 201, 208
Von Sternberg, Josef 23

W

"Waiting for the Sun" 93, 101, 102, 109, 135, 140
Warhol, Andy 84, 107, 132, 182
Waters, Muddy *iii*, 53, 82, 97, 104, 105
Werbelow, Mary *v*, 17, 32, 33, 44, 60, 73, 76, 102, 117, 140, 185, 193
Weiland, Scott 176
Weill, Kurt 25
West, Kanye 95, 180, 181
"When The Music's Over" 72, 82, 89, 155
Whisky A Go Go 67, 112
"Wild Child" 110, 114, 115
Wilde, Oscar 163, 164, 168

About the Author

Denise Sullivan is an American music journalist, historian, and author of music biographies as well as the critically acclaimed music-history book, *Keep on Pushing: Black Power Music From Blues to Hip Hop*. *Kirkus Reviews* calls it "A welcome exploration of how African American popular music became America's vernacular." *Library Journal* says, it's "Packed with informative details and commentary and those who are willing to give it the thoughtful reading it deserves will be rewarded."

A California-based freelance writer since 1991, from 2007-2011 she was a columnist and features writer for the online incarnation of *Crawdaddy!* the first US rock magazine to cover the music through a social and political lens in the 1960s. She has lived in San Francisco, Atlanta and Los Angeles, and has contributed to newspapers, books, magazines and web resources, from *The San Francisco Chronicle* and *The All Music Guide*, to *Rolling Stone*. Her books include T*he White Stripes: Sweethearts of the Blues* and *R.E.M. Talk About The Passion*.

"Denise Sullivan represents the insider intellectual stamina of rock 'n' roll journalism without the pomp and pretense. She is the past and future of the form, rolled into one uncanny style," says *Pop Matters*.

Find out more at her website: www.denisesullivan.com

CPSIA information can be obtained at www.ICGtesting.com
Printed in the USA
BVOW09*2007211114

376236BV00002B/4/P